new typo graphics

special collection of the best in contemporary typographic art

new typo graphics

The new faces of contemporary typography

P·I·E BOOKS

new typo graphics
The New Faces of Contemporary Typography

special collection of the best in contemporary typographic a

new typo graphics

Copyright ©1993 by P·I·E BOOKS

All right reserved. No part of this work may be reproduced in any form without written permission of the publisher.

First Published in Japan 1993 by P·I·E BOOKS
Villa Phoenix Suite 407, 4-14-6, Komagome, Toshima-ku,Tokyo 170, JAPAN
Tel: 03-3949-5010 Fax: 03-3949-5650

ISBN 4-938586-43-6

First Published in Germany 1993 by Nippan
Nippon Shuppan Hanbai Deutschland GmbH Krefelder Str. 85
D-40549 Düsseldorf 11 (Heerdt) GERMANY
Tel: 0211- 5048089 Fax: 0211- 5049326

ISBN 3-910052-32-0

Printed in Japan

Editorial Notes

Medium,Title of Work, Year of Completion,Submitor's Nationality

CD:Creative Director
AD:Art Director
TY:Typographer
D:Designer
P:Photographer
I:Illustrator
CW:CopyWriter
DF:Design Firm
CL:Client

The words "Company Limited" and "Incorporated" have been omitted from the credits in this book.
本文クレジット中,会社名については株式 (有限) 会社,Company Limited,Incorporated,等の表記 & 省略した。

ecial collection of the best in contemporary typographic art

new typo graphics

タイポグラフィは限りなく透明感のある光のようなものである。感じにくいものでとても美しいものなのだが日常生活ではときどき人は自然と見失ってしまう。僕らの生活はいつもタイポグラフィに溢れ、あたりまえのようにそこに存在しているからなのだと思う。

僕がタイポグラファーとなるきっかけとなった刺激の一つは「TM」(1) というスイスの印刷業界誌であった。1978年、僕はデザイン室の片隅で仕事の合間に「TM」を開いていた。なんということはない山家事のようだが、その当時「TM」は僕にとって"月間バイブル"といえる大切な存在であった。もう一つの刺激は紙の上ではなかった。テクノ・ミュージックが世の中に生まれようとしていた頃で、幸運にも僕はレコーディング・スタジオで、あらゆる音楽の可能性を追求していた3人と出会った。ひとりひとりの個性のぶつかりあいと見たこともないインストゥルメンツの中から新しいものを生み出していく、ものを作り出す姿勢とプロセスを真近にし感動した。自分も、好きなタイポグラフィに、このようなドキドキする事件をいつかもちこみたいと思っていた。まさしく音楽は今のタイポグラフィックな作業に類似する部分が多いと考えられる。特に音楽の世界でいわれるアレンジメント（編曲）に僕は強烈な興味をもつ。ひとつの楽譜からの表現方法は無限だ。どんな楽器を使うのか？どんな流れにするのか？きっと頭の中で想像するだけでウキウキするではないか。それに加えてクリエーターの間ではここのところマッキントッシュが共通な言語として身近になっていることからも、おそらくある種の新しい言語を作り出しているのだ。タイポグラフィはまさしくそのヴィジュアル化といってよいのではないだろうか。

今タイポグラフィは、ちょっと違った次元へ進もうとしている。活字を一つ一つ組んでいた時代とは違って、何か起きているのだろうか？もちろん、タイポグラファーと呼ばれる人の精神は、鉛の活字を自分の手で組み、オフセットのためのフィルム・ワーキングも自由に行い、その他の印刷テクニックを理解し駆使して何か伝達するものを紙の上に表現していくのが基本だ。現在、僕が在籍している学校がスイスのバーゼルにある。そこでインストラクションをしているウォルフガング・ワインガルトは1968年から学生のプロジェクトに実験タイ

TM, Dezember 1976: Die Struktur der weißen Fläche (das Alphabet und die Endpunkte)

TM 1976/12号・白い空間と造形の構成（アルファベットとポイント）

TM, December 1976: The structure of white space (the alphabet and the end-points)

special collection contemporary typographica

new graphics

004

1.「TM」
「TM」＝タイポグラフィッシュ・モナッツブレッターの略称で、スイスの印刷業界誌である。ワインガルトの作品群を見ることができるこの「TM」の強さは、シンプルなアイデアと見せ方にあると考えられる。常にスタートラインが白であり、今日多く見られる余計なノイズ（装飾）で成り立っているデザインとはひとつとしてない。つまりこの「TM」にあるノイズはタイポグラフィのエレメントとして処理され、全て生きているのである。表紙と内容のバランスを見てみるとそれらが同一レベルになっていること、そして各ページ違った印象を与えていることがわかる。例えば表紙つまり内向きの顔を写真と実写で美しくして、中身は表紙とはタイポグラフィックな模範なく、いつも同じ見せ方のバリケーションとは確実に異なっていて常に文字で正面きって見つめ合っている。

1.「TM」
TM is an abbreviation for Typographische Monatsblätter, the Swiss Typographic Monthly Magazine (Journal for Typographic Composition, Design, Communication, Printing and Production). In TM we can see the works of Weingart. The magazine's strength lies in its simple ideas and the straightforward way in which it presents typographical works. The stark, line-drawing basis of the designs are always shown against a blank white background. They never show a design that employs excessive noise (embellishment) of the sort we see all too often these days. In other words, any "noise" you see in TM is processed as a typographic element and is therefore effectively integrated into the function of the design. Looking at the balance between the front cover and the contents, we realize that everything is treated at the same level and yet each page produces a different impression. TM is certainly different from those ludicrous publications in which the front cover is adorned with pretty pictures and high production values, and whose contents bear no relation either typographically or stylistically with the publication cover. With TM one feels that the people involved in the publication have letters foremost in their minds at all times.

1.「TM」
"TM" ist die Abkürzung für Typographische Monatsblätter (Zeitschrift für Schriftsatz, Gestaltung, Sprache, Druck und Weiterverarbeitung) aus der Schweiz. In TM können wir die Arbeiten von Weingart sehen. Die Stärke der Zeitschrift liegt in der Einfachheit der Ideen und in der direkten ungekünstelten Art, in der die typographischen Designs präsentiert werden. Die schlichten, grundlinienbasierten Designs werden immer vor einem weißen, leeren Hintergrund gezeigt. Es wird nie ein Design vorgestellt, das mit exzessivem "Lärm" (Dekor) arbeitet, wie man es heute zu oft sieht. Mit anderen Worten, jeder "Lärm", der in TM zu sehen ist, wird als typographisches Element verarbeitet und daher wirkungsvoll in die Funktion des Designs integriert. Wenn wir das Gleichgewicht zwischen Titelseite und Inhalt betrachten, stellen wir fest, daß alles auf dem gleichen Niveau behandelt wird, und trotzdem jede Seite einen anderen Eindruck hervorruft. TM unterscheidet sich deutlich von den grotesken Publikationen, deren Titel sich mit bunten Bildern und hohem Produktionsaufwand schmücken, wo der Inhalt jedoch weder typographisch noch stilistisch in Relation zur Titelseite steht. Bei TM hat man den Eindruck, daß alle die an ihrer Veröffentlichung beteiligten, in erster Hinsicht und zu jeder Zeit Buchstaben im Kopf haben.

2. 実験タイポグラフィ
ワインガルトの実験タイポグラフィは世界的に有名である。基本的にはベーシック・タイポグラフィの延長線上にあると考えてよいが、無眼の可能性を持ち発展的なプロセスはモダン・タイポグラフィにはみかせない。マッキントッシュ登場以後は活版時代に比べると、ヴァリエーション作成がディスプレイ上で瞬時に確認できるようになったため、しやすくなった。僕が体感しているワインガルトの実験タイポグラフィは彼自身、そして彼の学生とのコラボレーションという形になっていてもよい。生きているタイポグラフィは自分をきちんと見つめることのできる世界一ある。僕にとって学校の「タイプショップ」は自分をきちんと見つめることのできる世界一の場所であり、このような上なる空間から生まれ出る実験タイポグラフィはまさしく実験なのだ。

ポグラフィ（2）を導入している。これは近代で重要なタイポグラフィの思想と技術をインテグレートして、感覚的な造形も生み出しながらタイポグラフィのあらゆる可能性をしらみつぶしに行うものである。僕にとってこれは何かを生み出すためのソースであり、音楽でいうサンプリングにちかいものだと解釈している。やはりワインガルトの実験タイポグラフィのベースには禁欲的なスイスタイポグラフィがある。このコンセプトは学内のプロジェクトから世界中に広がり、各地の色、あるいはいろいろなタイポグラファーの手で個性のようなものに置き換わり、少しづつ育ってきた。しかし今２つの大きな動向が起きていることは明らかである。それはタイポグラフィとしての大道、つまり少数の人により今世紀のほとんどを支配していた正確に情報を伝えるために視覚的な空間を操る方向性と、もう一つはカオス・タイポグラフィと呼ばれているものを意識的に生み出していく方向性である。以前はタイポグラフィという概念がそれほど一般的ではなかったため、単に前者のワクから外れるものばかりだった。しかし今、両方向が混在し僕らの前にある。その上タイポグラフィも音楽でいうワールド・ミュージックのように様々な国籍をもつ素材が自然と混ざり合う現状にあり、だからこそ文字に向かい僕らは常にきちんと目を開いて取り組んでいかなければならないのである。もう一つ興味深いのは、文字に関する材料はいつの時代にもいろいろな所にころがっていることである。それは、タイポグラフィの限界（3）を注意深く観察することにより、次のステップが見えてくる。また作り出すことができるのである。

おそらくこれから登場する作品群は、いわゆる東洋と西洋の接点ということばで結論がでるのではなく、一般化され、とにかく"おでんの煮汁"のようなもので、つまり画像上写真もイラストも、もちろん文字も同等のレベルで扱われる状態のところにまでもってきている。そこでまだまだ可能性があるグラフィックをタイポグラフィという扉を開くことにより、何か新しいものを呼び起こしたい気分でいっぱいにさせるのだ。この本を開くにあたって、一度目はペラペラと目を通す感じで見てほしい。二度目は、一つ一つに何かタイポグラフィのキーを見つけ、細部に探りを入れてほしい。

小泉均プロフィール
1958年東京生まれ。タイポグラファー。1990年から日本人としての初のスイスでのアルマイネ・ゲベルベシューレ・バーゼルへ入学し、アドヴァンスド・クラスでヴォルフガング・ヴァインガルトとのプロジェクトを続けている。現在、長岡造形大学での日本語を中心とした実験タイポグラフィの計画をスタートさせている。教育プロセス上でのマッキントッシュ導入方法と、身近なテーマからの視覚的なコミュニケーションの手段を探る。

the best ... typographic art

LICHT PROJECT No.12 by Hitoshi Koizumi

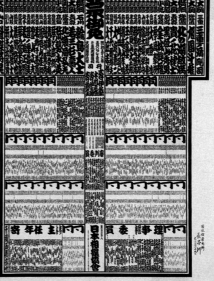

大相撲の番付表－長体変形の限界（手書き文字）Sumo ranking chart: limits of horizontal compression (hand-written characters) Sumo-Rangliste: Grenzen horizontaler Kompression (handgeschriebene Schriftzeichen)

2. Experimental Typography

Weingart's experimental typography is known worldwide. Essentially, one can consider it an extension of "basic typography", but it has become a vital part of modern typography with its infinite possibilities in design and progressive processes. The arrival of Macintosh computers in design has greatly facilitated this movement. Now, the creation of variations on a graphic theme can be instantly verified on the display. Weingart's experimental typography is really a collaborative effort between Weingart himself and his students. Live typography is a fusion, wherein actual people who live and breathe interact with each other and with the principles of design. For me, the "type shop" inside the school is the only place in this world where I can take a good look at myself. The experimental typography that emanates from that unique space is experimental in the true sense of the word.

2. Experimentellen Typographie

Weingarts experimentelle Typographie ist weltbekannt. Man kann sie im wesentlichen als eine Erweiterung der 'grundsätzlichen Typographie' betrachten. Sie wurde aber, mit ihren unendlichen Möglichkeiten und fortschreitenden Prozessen, zu einem lebendigen Teil der modernen Typographie. Der Einzug des Macintosh-Computers ins Design hat diesen Schritt sehr erleichtert. Jetzt können die Variationen eines graphischen Themas sofort auf dem Monitor überprüft werden. Weingarts experimentelle Typographie, in die ich unmittelbar verwickelt bin, ist in Wirklichkeit eine Zusammenarbeit zwischen Weingart und seinen Studenten. Lebendige Typographie, die leben und atmen, miteinander und mit den Prinzipien des Designs interagieren. Für mich ist der "Schriftladen" in der Schule der einzige Platz auf der Welt, in dem ich einen guten Blick auf mich selbst werfen kann. Die experimentelle Typographie, die von diesem einzigartigen Ort ausstrahlt, ist experimentell im wahrsten Sinne des Wortes.

3. タイポグラフィの限界

注意深くものを見る、タイポグラフィにとって最高の方法論である。一言で語ることはできないが、どんな印刷物にも可能性はある。例えば単位面積当りの情報量について考えてみると、当然情報量を増やせば文字が小さくなる。このような条件では僕らは何を限界としてみているのか？世界中でいったいどこでも文字の空間が狭くなる。このような条件では僕らは何を限界としてみているのか？世界中でいったいどこでも文字の空間が狭くなる。そのアウトラインから生まれる造形とタイポグラフィのエレメントに関しての限界へ挑戦することは、文字の瀬戸際に立っているような感じがする。

3. Limits of Typography

Looking at objects with great care, is the essential methodology of good typography. Although it is impossible to talk about it in simple terms, all printed matter has possibilities. Consider the amount of typographical information you can compress into, let's say, a square inch of space. Naturally, if you increase the amount of information, the point size of the characters will have to be reduced and the space between the characters will have to be correspondingly reduced. In terms of this sort of restriction, what should our limits be? All over the world at any given time, methods for this pursuit – the increase of information communicated – constantly change, and as a result the means of expression change as well. Where we meet the limitations of typographical elements, we stand right at the boundary between recognizable characters and pure shape.

3. Grenzen der Typographie

Die Objekte mit großer Sorgfalt zu betrachten, ist die grundlegende Methode guter Typographie. Obwohl es unmöglich ist, darüber in einfachen Worten zu sprechen, hat alles Gedruckte seine Möglichkeiten. Bedenken Sie z.B. die Menge an typographischer Information, die in einen Quadratzentimeter komprimiert werden kann. Um so höher die Informationsmenge, um so mehr muß der Schriftgrad, sowie auch der Raum zwischen den Zeichen, verkleinert werden. In Anbetracht dieser Art von Einschränkungen, was sollen da unsere Grenzen sein? Überall auf der Welt andern sich andauernd die Methoden mitgeteilte Information zu steigern, und als Resultat andern sich die Ausdrucksformen genauso. Wenn wir auf die Beschränkungen der typographischen Elemente stoßen, stehen wir direkt an der Grenze zwischen erkennbaren Typen und der reinen Gestalt.

In a way, typography is like light in that it can be perfectly transparent. It holds within it the sublime contradiction of being beautiful and at the same time invisible. For most people most of the time it is taken utterly for granted, like the natural environment. I think this is because our lives are overflowing with typography and so typography has become the presumed backdrop of our visual landscape.

One of the things that inspired me to become a typographer in the first place was the Swiss magazine "TM". (1) Back in 1978, while working in a design studio I took advantage of free moments between jobs to pore over the pages of that magazine. Even though it might seem to have been a minor occurrence, at that point in my life, TM played such an important role that I thought of it as a sort of monthly Bible installment.

Another thing that motivated me early on was something not found on paper. This was around the time when musicians were trying to bring techno-music to the attention of the world. Fortunately for me, I met three daring musicians who were exploring new musical territory at a local recording studio. They were giving birth to something totally unheard of, employing musical instruments that I had never seen before. They were exploiting the contrasts and even the confrontational engagements of their strong personalities to create something extraordinary. It was a seminal experience for me; I was powerfully affected by their creative attitude and the inventive processes through which they did their work.

I wanted this kind of thrill in my work. I began to wonder how I could bring a similar excitement, a similar creative dynamic into typography. After all, there are ways in which music has much in common with current typographic work. In particular, I have a strong interest in musical arrangement because it allows for an infinite number of ways to express a single score. What instruments to use? How should it be presented? Musicians become excited just thinking about the possibilities.

Macintosh computers now have become a kind of common tool for all kinds of creative processes, a means by which creative people in all fields can communicate with a common language. With this new medium we are creating a new vocabulary as well, and typography is at the heart of it all.

At present, typography is poised to vault into a new dimension. We are long past the days when typographers had to painstakingly put in place each hand-crafted letter with their own fingers, and it seems now that anything is possible. Of course, to achieve the ultimate goal of expressing something through typography on paper, it is still necessary to have a complete mastery and understanding of printing techniques, from placing lead type by hand to the processes of film work for offset printing.

The school at which I am now enrolled is located in Basel, Switzerland. Wolfgang Weingart, who is an instructor there, first introduced the concept of "experimental typography" (2) for student projects in 1968. This entails the idea of integrating all important modern typographical ideas and techniques

TM 1976/12号・写真、ダイアグラムその他のエレメントの構成

TM, December 1976: Composition of elements including photography and diagrams

TM, Dezember 1976: Komposition von Elementen, einschließlich Photographien und Diagrammen

special collect ... in contemporary typographic a

new ... graphics

1. "TM"

TM is an abbreviation for Typographische Monatsblätter, the Swiss Typographic Monthly Magazine (Journal for Typographic Composition, Design, Communication, Printing and Production). In TM we can see the works of Weingart. The magazine's strength lies in its simple ideas and the straightforward way in which it presents typographical works. The stark, line-drawing basis of the designs are always shown against a blank white background. They never show a design that employs excessive *noise* (embellishment) of the sort we see all too often these days. In other words, any "noise" you see in TM is processed as a typographic element and is therefore effectively integrated into the function of the design. Looking at the balance between the front cover and the contents, we realize that everything is treated at the same level and yet each page produces a different impression. TM is certainly different from those ludicrous publications in which the front cover is adorned with pretty pictures and high production values, and whose contents bear no relation either typographically or stylistically with the cover. With TM, one feels that the people involved in the publication have letters foremost in their minds at all times.

1. "TM"

"TM" ist die Abkürzung für Typografische Monatsblätter (Zeitschrift für Schriftsatz, Gestaltung, Sprache, Druck und Weiterverarbeitung) aus der Schweiz. In TM können wir die Arbeiten von Weingart sehen. Die Stärke der Zeitschrift liegt in der Einfachheit der Ideen und in der direkten, ungekünstelten Art, in der die typographischen Arbeiten präsentiert werden. Die schlichten, grundlinienbasierten Designs werden immer vor einem weißen, leeren Hintergrund gezeigt. Es wird nie ein Design vorgestellt, das mit exzessivem "Lärm" (Dekor) arbeitet, wie man es heute zu oft sieht. Mit anderen Worten, jeder "Lärm", der in TM zu sehen ist, wird als typographisches Element verarbeitet und daher wirkungsvoll in die Funktion des Designs integriert. Wenn wir das Gleichgewicht zwischen Titelseite und Inhalt betrachten, stellen wir fest, daß alles auf dem gleichen Niveau behandelt wird, und trotzdem jede Seite einen anderen Eindruck hervorruft. TM unterscheidet sich deutlich von den grotesken Publikationen, deren Titel sich mit bunten Bildern und hohem Produktionsaufwand schmücken, wo der Inhalt jedoch weder typographisch noch stilistisch in Relation zur Titelseite steht. Bei TM hat man den Eindruck, daß all die an ihrer Veröffentlichung beteiligten, in erster Hinsicht und zu jeder Zeit Buchstaben im Kopf haben.

while exploring all the possibilities of typography to the limits of what can be signified by shape and form. This is a creative well-spring for me and what I draw from it , I see as a form of the "sampling" used in music.

The basis of Weingart's experimental typography lies in the stoic Swiss lineage of typography. The concept of experimental typography began as a school project but has grown and spread all over the world. The diversity of the experiment now reflects various local colors and the sensibilities of individual typographers and thus has broadened into a universal discourse. However, two major movements are now emerging in the field. One carries on in the direction that has been governing typography for most of this century, in which a relatively small number of people - the professionals of foundry typography - have had control over virtually all of the visual space where information is communicated. In the other more current movement, people are consciously trying to create so-called "chaos" typography. The principles of classical typography have not been well understood beyond the type caster's rack until recently, so whatever could not be fitted into the framework of the first movement was considered a mere aberration. Today, however, particularly with the advent of desktop publishing, this second direction is more clearly defined and each of the movements is beginning to reflect the strengths of the other. Moreover, typography has reached a stage in which graphic material from various cultures can not only coexist but come together harmoniously as they do, for example, in "World Music." This heterogeneous situation demands of us that we be especially vigilant and clear-eyed when it comes to letters and that the creators of typography approach their work with absolutely clear intentions. One more thing I find interesting is that ideas for characters can be found everywhere and in any given era. A typographer on the path to originality can acquire a clear view of the next step to be taken by carefully observing the "limits of typography." (3) By doing this, the typographer may blaze the path himself, for others to follow.

I doubt that the works of typography that you will see in this book can be accurately characterized by any glib expression such as "The meeting of East and West." Some of these works are like a broth, containing all sorts of creative juices and ingredients. In the end, it doesn't matter where a particular ingredient comes from because it gets subsumed in the broth. Visual images of all kinds, photos, illustrations and characters, are all elements that may be regarded on an equal plane. Typography is a window through which one can look into a world of graphics and see many unexplored possibilities. When we open it, we are filled with the urge to discover something new.

When opening this book, on the first time through, I suggest that you just scan the pages; then on each subsequent perusal, probe into the details of the individual typographical works and try to find the key to each design.

A Profile of Hitoshi Koizumi, Typographer.
Born in Tokyo in 1958. In 1990 he entered the Allgemeine Gewerbeschule in Basel, Switzerland -- the first Japanese to be admitted. At the advanced class at this institution, Koizumi started a collaborative project with Wolfgang Weingart that is still on-going. Currently, he is working on a plan to implement experimental typography in Japanese characters at the Nagaoka Institute of Design. He is pursuing a study of possible methodologies for introducing the Macintosh computer into the educational process as a means for visual communication dealing with everyday themes.

surfaces using a plane tool (Macintosh) TM, April 1982: Grenzen der Formen

erstellt durch Tate flächen, unter Verwendung

eines einfachen Werkzeuges (Macintosh)

LICHT PROJECT No.24 by Hitoshi Koizumi

TM 1982/4 号 ペイントのツールによる版面の造形の限界 (MAC゛: TM, April 1982: limits in shapes created with plate

2. Experimental Typography
Weingart's experimental typography is known worldwide. Essentially, one can consider it an extension of "basic typography", but it has become a vital part of modern typography with its infinite possibilities and progressive processes. The arrival of Macintosh computers in design has greatly facilitated this movement. Now, the creation of variations on a graphic theme can be instantly verified on the display. Weingart's experimental typography with which I am involved is in reality a collaborative effort between Weingart himself and his students. Live typography is a fusion, wherein actual people who live and breathe interact with each other and with the principles of design. For me, the "type shop" inside the school is the only place in this world where I can take a good look at myself. The experimental typography that emanates from that unique space is experimental in the true sense of the word.

2. Experimentelle Typographie
Weingarts experimentelle Typographie ist weltbekannt. Man kann sie im wesentlichen als eine Erweiterung der "grundsätzlichen Typographie" betrachten. Sie wurde aber, mit ihren unendlichen Möglichkeiten und fortschreitenden Prozessen, zu einem lebendigen Teil der modernen Typographie. Der Einzug des Macintosh-Computers ins Design hat diesen Schritt sehr erleichtert. Jetzt können die Variationen eines graphischen Themas sofort auf dem Monitor überprüft werden. Weingarts experimentelle Typographie, in die ich unmittelbar verwickelt bin, ist in Wirklichkeit eine Zusammenarbeit zwischen Weingart und seinen Studenten. Lebendige Typographie ist eine Fusion, bei der leibhaftige Menschen die leben und atmen, miteinander und mit den Prinzipien des Designs interagieren. Für mich ist der "Schriftladen" in der Schule der einzige Platz auf der Welt, in dem ich einen guten Blick auf mich selbst werfen kann. Die experimentelle Typographie, die von diesem einzigartigen Ort ausstrahlt, ist experimentell im wahrsten Sinne des Wortes.

2 タイポグラフィの限界
注意深くものを見る、タイポグラフィにとって最大の方法論である。一言で語ることはできないが、どんな印刷物にも制限はある。例えば紙面面積当たりの情報量について考えてみると、当然情報量を増やせば文字が小さくなる、文字と文字の空間が狭くなる、このような条件で情報を増やしてゆくのか世界中のどこでも最末の方法が変わり表現が違ってくる。その枠に隠れたタイポグラフィのエレメントに関しての限界へ沈着させることはアクションとから生まれる造形と文字の瀬戸際にいるような感じがする。

3. Limits of Typography
Looking at objects with great care, is the essential methodology of good typography. Although it is impossible to talk about it in simple terms, all printed matter has possibilities. Consider the amount of typographical information you can compress into, let's say, a square inch of space. Naturally, if you increase the amount of information, the point size of the characters will have to be reduced and the space between the characters will have to be correspondingly reduced. In terms of this sort of restriction, what should our limits be? All over the world at any given time, methods for this pursuit -- the increase of information communicated -- constantly change, and as a result the means of expression change as well. When we meet the limitations of typographical elements, we stand right at the boundary between recognizable characters and pure shape.

3. Grenzen der Typographie
Die Objekte mit großer Sorgfalt zu betrachten, ist die grundlegende Methode guter Typographie. Obwohl es unmöglich ist, darüber in einfachen Worten zu sprechen, hat alles Gedruckte seine Möglichkeiten. Bedenken Sie z.B. die Menge an typographischer Information, die in einen Quadratzentimeter komprimiert werden kann. Um so höher die Informationsmenge, um so mehr muß der Schriftgrad sowie auch der Raum zwischen den Zeichen, verkleinert werden. In Anbetracht dieser Art von Einschränkungen, was sollen die Limitationen sein? Überall auf der Welt ändern sich andauernd die vielfältige Information zu steigern, die Methoden. Als Resultat ändern sich die Ausdrucksmethoden ebenso. Wenn wir an die Grenzen der typographischen Elemente stoßen, stehen wir direkt an der Grenze zwischen erkennbaren Typen und der reinen Gestalt.

Die Typographie ist in gewisser Weise vergleichbar mit dem Licht - sie kann völlig transparent sein. Sie birgt in sich den sublimen Wiederspruch, gleichzeitig schön und unsichtbar zu sein. Zum größten Teil der Zeit, wird sie für die meisten Menschen als etwas Selbstverständliches hingenommen, so wie auch unsere natürliche Umgebung. Das liegt, glaube ich, daran, daß unser Leben mit Typographie überläuft, und die Typographie somit zu einem vorausgesetzten Hintergrund unserer visuellen Landschaft wurde.

Eine der Dinge, die mich an erster Stelle dazu anregten Typograph zu werden, war die schweizer Zeitschrift "TM".(1)   Als ich 1978 in einem Designstudio arbeitete, nutzte ich die freie Zeit zwischen den Aufträgen, um die Seiten dieser Zeitschrift zu überdenken. Obwohl es den Anschein einer Nebensache haben mag, spielte TM zu dieser Zeit in meinem Leben eine so wichtige Rolle, daß ich sie für eine Art Bibel in monatlichen Raten hielt.

Etwas anderes, was mich zusätzlich von Anfang an motivierte, ist nicht auf Papier zu finden. Etwa zu dieser Zeit versuchten einige Musiker, "techno-music" in der Öffentlichkeit bekanntzumachen. Zu meinem großen Glück hatte ich die Gelegenheit, drei unternehmungslustige Musiker kennenzulernen, die in einem örtlichen Aufnahmestudio musikalisches Neuland betraten. Sie schufen etwas bis dahin Ungehörtes und verwendeten Musikinstrumente, die ich noch nie vorher gesehen hatte. Sie nutzten die Kontraste und sogar die konfrontativen Einsätze ihrer starken Persönlichkeiten, um etwas Außergewöhnliches zu produzieren. Dies war eine prägende Erfahrung für mich; ich wurde stark angeregt von der kreativen Vorgehensweise und dem erfindungsreichen Entwicklungsprozeß, die ihrer Arbeit zugrunde lagen.

Ich wollte diese Art von Spannung in meiner Arbeit haben. Ich überlegte mir, wie ich eine ähnliche Aufregung, eine ähnliche kreative Dynamik, in die Typographie einbringen könnte. Schließlich hat Musik viele Gemeinsamkeiten mit gegenwärtiger typographischer Arbeit. Ich habe ein besonderes Interesse an musikalischen Arrangements, da sie eine unendliche Anzahl von Möglichkeiten bieten, eine bestimmte Partitur zu interpretieren. Welche Instrumente sollen verwendet werden, wie das Ganze präsentieren? Musiker werden alleine schon von den Gedanken an die vielfältigen Möglichkeiten begeistert.

Macintosh-Computer sind zu einer Art geläufigem Werkzeug geworden für jede Art von kreativen Prozessen, und zu einem Mittel, wodurch kreative Menschen in allen Bereichen in einer gemeinsamen Sprache kommunizieren können. Mit diesem neuen Medium schaffen wir gleichzeitig ein neues Vokabular – und die Typographie ist das Herzstück des Ganzen.

Gegenwärtig ist die Typographie in einer Art Schwebezustand, um in eine neue Dimension vorstoßen zu können. Die Zeiten, in denen ein Schriftsetzer jeden handgegossenen Buchstaben mit den eigenen Händen plazierte sind lange vorbei, und es scheint mittlerweile, als ob alles möglich sei. Natürlich, um die übergeordnete Aufgabe - etwas auf dem Papier durch Typographie zum Ausdruck zu bringen -zu erfüllen, ist es immer noch nötig die Drucktechniken zu meistern und voll zu verstehen, vom Handsetzen der Lettern bis zu den Vorgängen der Filmherstellung für den Offset-Druck.

Die Schule an der ich zur Zeit bin ist in Basel, Schweiz. Dort lehrt Wolfgang Weingart, der das Konzept der "experimentellen Typographie" erstmals 1968 für Studienprojekte entwickelt hatte.(2) Es beinhaltet den Gedanken, alle wichtigen modernen typographischen Gedanken und Techniken zu

TM 1976/12号・スクリプトを重ねるフィルムワーク的構成

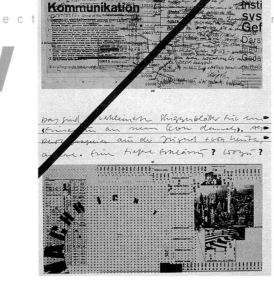

new graphics

TM, December 1976: Film work composition in which scripts are overlaid

TM, Dezember 1976: Komposition von Filmarbeiten,
in der Schriften übereinandergelegt sind

1. "TM"

TM is an abbreviation for Typographische Monatsblätter, the Swiss Typographic Monthly Magazine (Journal for Typographic Composition. Design. Communication. Printing and Production). In TM we can see the works of Weingart. The magazine's strength lies in its simple ideas and the straightforward way in which it presents typographical works. The stark, line-drawing basis of the designs are always shown against a blank white background. They never show a design that employs excessive noise (embellishment) of the sort we see all too often these days. In other words, any "noise" you see in TM is processed as a typographic element and is therefore effectively integrated into the function of the design. Looking at the balance between the front cover and the contents, we realize that everything is treated at the same level and yet each part produces a different impression. TM is certainly different from those ludicrous publications in which the front cover is adorned with pretty pictures and high production values, and whose contents bear no relation either typographically or stylistically with the cover. With TM, one feels that the people involved in the publication have letters foremost in their minds at all times.

1. "TM"

"TM" ist die Abkürzung für Typografische Monatsblätter (Zeitschrift für Schriftsatz, Gestaltung, Sprache, Druck und Weiterverarbeitung) aus der Schweiz. In TM können wir die Arbeiten von Weingart sehen. Die Stärke der Zeitschrift liegt in der Einfachheit der Ideen und in der direkten, ungekünstelten Art, in der die typographischen Arbeiten präsentiert werden. Die schlichten, grundlinienbasierten Designs werden immer vor einem weißen, leeren Hintergrund gezeigt. Es wird nie ein Design vorgestellt, das mit exzessivem "Lärm" (Dekor) arbeitet, wie man es heute zu oft sieht. Mit anderen Worten, jeder "Lärm", der in TM zu sehen ist, wird als typographisches Element verarbeitet und ist daher wirkungsvoll in die Funktion des Designs integriert. Wenn wir das Gleichgewicht zwischen Titelseite und Inhalt betrachten, stellen wir fest, daß alles auf dem gleichen Niveau behandelt wird, und trotzdem jede Seite einen anderen Eindruck hervorruft. TM unterscheidet sich deutlich von den grotesken Publikationen, deren Titel sich mit bunten Bildern und hohem Produktionsaufwand schmücken, wo der Inhalt jedoch weder typographisch noch stilistisch in Relation zur Titelseite steht. Bei TM hat man den Eindruck, daß alle die an ihrer Veröffentlichung beteiligen, in erster Hinsicht und zu jeder Zeit Buchstaben im Kopf haben.

integrieren, und gleichzeitig alle Möglichkeiten der Typographie zu erforschen, bis an die Grenze dessen, was durch Form und Gestalt ausgedrückt werden kann. Für mich ist dies ein kreativer Jungbrunnen, und was ich aus ihm schöpfe, sehe ich als eine Art "sampling" gebräuchlich in der Musik.

Die Basis für Weingarts experimentelle Typographie wurzelt in der stoischen schweizer Tradition der Typographie. Das Konzept der experimentellen Typographie begann als ein Studienprojekt, aber es hat diesen Rahmen gesprengt und sich in aller Welt verbreitet. Die Unterschiedlichkeit des Experimentes reflektiert heute verschiedenes Lokalkolorit sowie die Empfindsamkeit der einzelnen Typographen, und hat sich so in einen universellen Diskurs ausgeweitet. Dennoch sind zwei Hauptströmungen deutlich zu unterscheiden. Eine setzt die Entwicklung fort, die für die Typographie dieses Jahrhundert meist ausschlaggebend war, in der eine vergleichsweise kleine Zahl von Leuten, die professionellen Typographen der Schriftanstalten, praktisch die Kontrolle hatten über den ganzen visuellen Bereich in dem Information mitgeteilt wird. In der anderen, mehr aktuelleren Strömung, wird bewußt versucht, eine sogenannte "Chaos-Typographie" zu schaffen. Bis vor kurzem wurden die Prinzipien der klassischen Typographie über die Setzkästen hinaus kaum verstanden, und so wurde alles, was nicht den Prinzipien der erstgenannten Bewegung folgte, als eine Verirrung angesehen. Mit dem Einzug des Desktop-Publishing aber, ist heute die zweite Richtung klarer definiert, und jede der beiden Strömung fängt an, die Stärken der anderen zu reflektieren. Darüber hinaus hat die Typographie heute eine Entwicklungsstufe erreicht, in der graphisches Material aus verschiedenen Kulturen nicht nur nebeneinander existieren, sondern sogar in Einklang zusammengebracht werden kann, wie es zum Beispiel auch in der "World Music" der Fall ist. Diese heterogene Situation verlangt von uns, daß wir besonders wach und scharfäugig sind, wenn es um Schrift geht und das Alle, die Typographie gestalten, an ihre Arbeit mit absolut klarer Zielsetzung herangehen. Außerdem finde ich es interessant, daß Ideen für Buchstaben überall und in jeder Zeit gefunden werden können. Ein Typograph auf dem Weg zur Originalität kann sich eine klare Vorstellung von dem nächsten notwendigen Schritt machen, indem er die "Grenzen der Typographie" sorgfältig beobachtet.(3) Auf diese Art und Weise kann er selbst den Weg freisprengen, den andere dann folgen können.

Ich bezweifle, daß die Typographiearbeiten, die Sie in diesem Buch finden werden, mit einem oberflächlichem Ausdruck wie "Das Treffen von Ost und West" bezeichnet werden können. Zwar sind einige dieser Arbeiten tatsächlich wie eine Art Schmelztiegel oder Gebräu, das allerlei kreative Säfte und Zutaten enthält. Letzendlich ist es aber unwichtig, woher eine bestimmte Zutat kommt, da sie im Gebräu aufgeht. Visuelle Darstellungen jeglicher Art, Photos, Illustrationen und Buchstaben sind alles Elemente, die auf einer gleichen Ebene betrachtet werden können. Die Typographie ist ein Fenster, durch das man in eine Welt der Graphik schauen kann, und viele unerforschte Möglichkeiten sieht. Wenn wir es öffnen, erfüllt uns der Wunsch etwas Neues zu entdecken.

Beim ersten Öffnen des Buches schlage ich vor, daß Sie nur die Seiten überfliegen. Dann können Sie bei jedem weiteren Durchsehen in die Details der einzelnen typographischen Arbeiten eindringen, und versuchen den Schlüssel zu jedem Design zu finden.

Ein Profil von Hitoshi Koizumi, Typograph.

Geboren in Tokyo, 1958. 1990 immatrikulierte er sich als erster Japaner in der Allgemeinen Gewerbeschule in Basel, Schweiz. Dort fing er in der höheren Klasse ein kollaboratives Projekt mit Wolfgang Weingart an, welches bis heute andauert. Derzeit arbeitet er am Nagaoka Institut für Gestaltung an einem Plan, experimentelle Typographie in japanischen Schriftzeichen einzuführen. Er untersucht außerdem mögliche Methoden, den Macintosh-Computer in den Ausbildungsprozeß als ein Mittel visueller Kommunikation einzuführen, welches mit alltäglichen Themen umgehen kann.

IM, December 1976: limits of legibility (screen effects and horizontal lines)

TM 1976/12号 可読性に対する限界（スクリーン・エフェクトと罫線）

12 1976	Typographische Monatsblätter	Schweizer Grafische Mitteilungen	Revue suisse de l'Imprimerie
TM		SGM	RSI

Ist diese Typografie noch zu retten?
Oder leben wir auf dem Mond? Is This Typography Worth Supporting, Or Do We Live On The Moon?

TM, Dezember 1976: Grenzen der Lesbarkeit

(Bildschirmrastereffekte und horizontale Linien)

LICHT PROJECT No.41 by Hitoshi Koizumi

2. Experimental Typography

Weingart's experimental typography is known worldwide. Essentially, one can consider it an extension of "basic typography", but it has become a vital part of modern typography with its infinite possibilities and progressive processes. The arrival of Macintosh computers in design has greatly facilitated this movement. Now, the creation of variations on a graphic theme can be instantly verified on the display. Weingart's experimental typography with which I am involved is in reality a collaborative effort between Weingart himself and his students. Live typography is a fusion, wherein actual people who live and breathe interact with each other and with the principles of design. For me, the "type shop" inside the school is the only place in this world where I can take a good look at myself. The experimental typography that emanates from that unique space is experimental in the true sense of the word.

2. Experimentellen Typographie

Weingarts experimentelle Typographie ist weltbekannt. Man kann sie im wesentlichen als eine Erweiterung der "grundsätzlichen Typographie" betrachten. Sie wurde aber, mit ihren unendlichen Möglichkeiten und fortschreitenden Prozessen, zu einem lebendigen Teil der modernen Typographie. Der Einzug des Macintosh-Computers in Design hat diesen Schritt sehr erleichtert. Jetzt können die Variationen eines graphischen Themas sofort auf dem Monitor überprüft werden. Weingarts experimentelle Typographie, in die ich unmittelbar verwickelt bin, ist in Wirklichkeit eine Zusammenarbeit zwischen Weingart und seinen Studenten. Lebendige Typographie ist eine Fusion, bei der leibhaftige Menschen die leben und atmen, miteinander und mit den Prinzipien des Designs interagieren. Für mich ist der "Schriftladen" in der Schule der einzige Platz auf der Welt, in dem ich einen guten Blick auf mich selbst werfen kann. Die experimentelle Typographie, die von diesem einzigartigen Ort ausstrahlt, ist experimentell im wahrsten Sinne des Wortes.

3. タイポグラフィの限界

主題に大きな注意を払って物事を見る、タイポグラフィにとって最大の方法論である。一言で言うことはできないが、どんな印刷物にも可能性はある。例えば可能性は紙面に占めることについて考えてみよう。そこに、紙面の情報量を圧縮することができるとしても、文字と文字の間のスペースの広がりを切りつめることになる。果たしてどれほどまで情報量を減少できるのだろうか？あらゆるところにある無限の世界の中で、その場所における制限という点で減らすことになることは、この種の探求に関して制限される。情報の増加にともなって、伝達のための手段もまた絶えず変化する。

3. Limits of Typography

Looking at objects with great care, is the essential methodology of good typography. Although it is impossible to talk about it in simple terms, all printed matter has possibilities. Consider the amount of typographical information you can compress into, let's say, a square inch of space. Naturally, if you increase the amount of information, the point size of the characters will have to be reduced and the space between the characters will have to be correspondingly reduced. In terms of this sort of restriction, what should our limits be? All over the world at any given time, methods for this pursuit - as the means of information communicated - constantly change - and as a result the means of expression change as well. When we meet the limitations of typographical elements, we stand right at the boundary between recognizable characters and pure shape.

3. Grenzen der Typographie

Die Objekte mit großer Sorgfalt zu betrachten, ist die grundlegende Methode guter Typographie. Obwohl es unmöglich ist, darüber in einfachen Worten zu sprechen, hat alles Gedruckte seine Möglichkeiten. Bedenken Sie z. B. die Menge an typographischer Information, die in einen Quadratzentimeter komprimiert werden kann. Um so höher die Informationsmenge, um so mehr muß der Schriftgrad, sowie auch der Raum zwischen den Zeichen, verkleinert werden. In Anbetracht dieser Art von Einschränkungen, was sollen da unsere Grenzen sein? Überall auf der Welt ändern sich andauernd die Methoden mitgeteilte Information zu steigern, und als Resultat ändern sich die Ausdrucksformen genauso. Wenn wir auf die Beschränkungen der typographischen Elemente stoßen, stehen wir direkt an der Grenze zwischen erkennbaren Typen und der reinen Gestalt.

Posters ポスター

Snap Design Promotiona Poster Series　USA 1992

CD:Fred Rolito　AD,D:Raul Cabra　P:Cesar Rubio

DF:Snap Design　CL:Snap Design

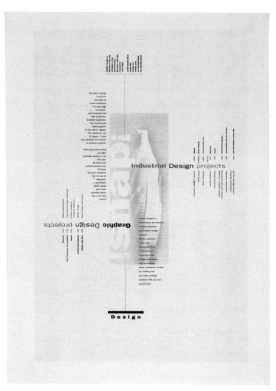

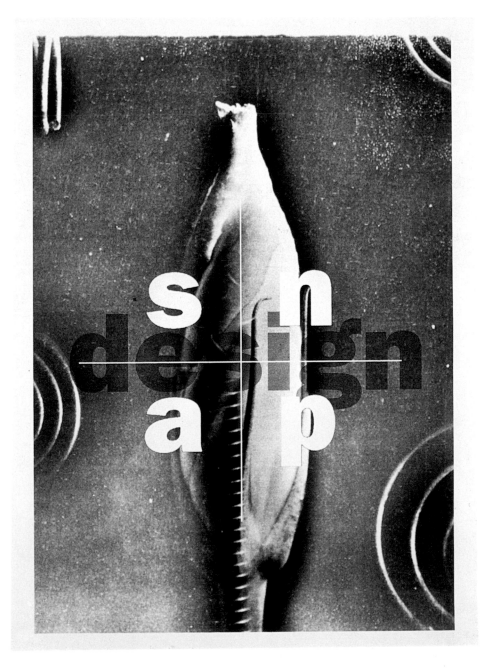

Book 本

Cranbrook Design "The New Discourse" USA 1991

CD:Robert Janvigian

CL:Rizzoli International

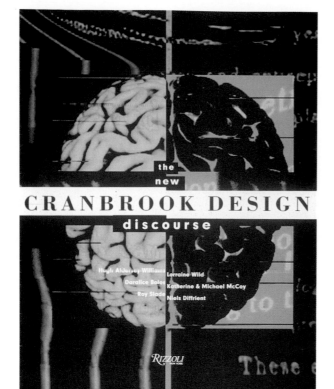

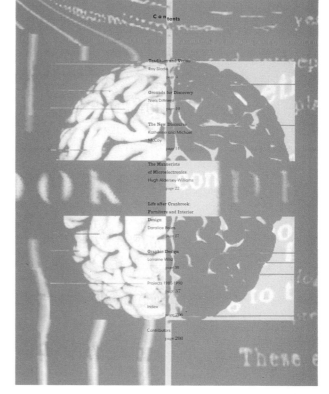

Contents

Cranbrook is like no other institution in the United States. It is part artists' colony, part school, part museum and part design laboratory, and it has never allowed its students to be bound by the narrow lines separating the various design disciplines...the effect of Cranbrook and its graduates and faculty on the physical environment of this country has been profound. . . . . For Cranbrook, surely more than any other institution, has the right to think of itself as synonymous with contemporary American design.

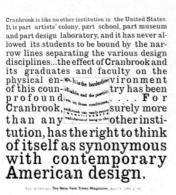

Paul Goldberger, **The New York Times Magazine**, April 8, 1984 p. 43

The work presented in the following pages includes studio assignments, independent studio projects, professional work by alumni, and professional work by Cranbrook faculty. The names of Cranbrook students, graduates, and faculty who were involved in the projects are presented in bold-face type.

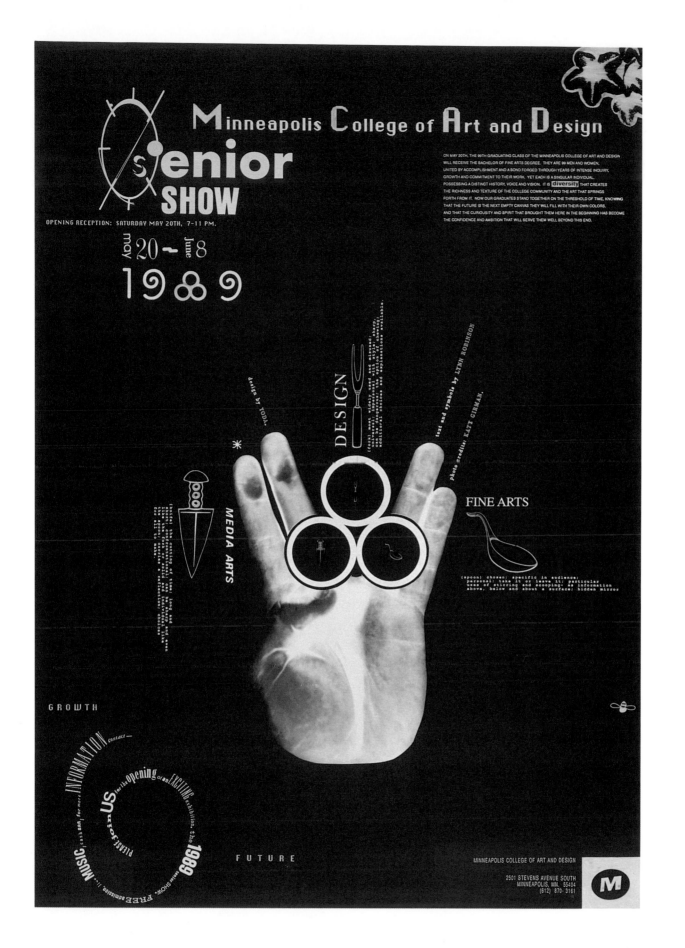

Poster ポスター

MCAD Senior Show　USA 1989

AD:Jan Jancourt　D:Timorse　P:Katy Girman　I:Lynn Robinson

CW:Kyia Downing　DF:Coloured Hard　CL:Minneapolis College of Art & Design

Poster ポスター

Melbourne Internationa Film Festival Australia 1992

AD,D:Andrew Hoyne P:Rob Blackburn

DF:Andrew Hoyne Design CL:Melbourne Film Festival

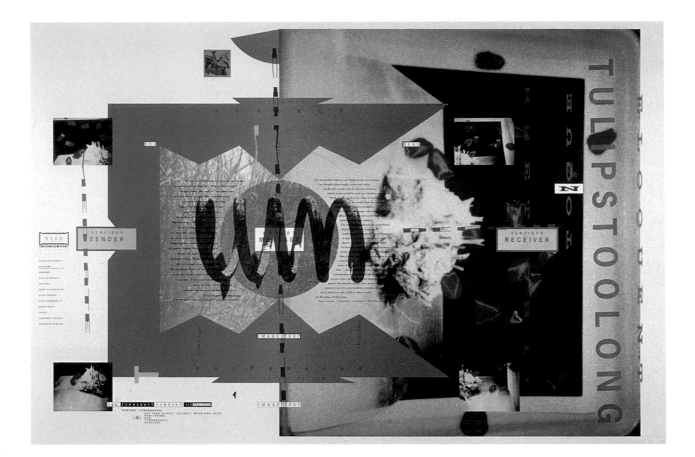

Poster ポスター

Two Lips Too Long USA 1989
D:Allen Hori P:Allen Hori
DF:Cranbrook Academy of Art, Department of Design CL:Typocraft Printing

Poster ポスター

Melbourne Film Festival Australia 1991
AD,D:Andrew Hoyne I:Pacquita Maher, Andrew Hoyne
DF:Andrew Hoyne Design CL:Melbourne Film Festival

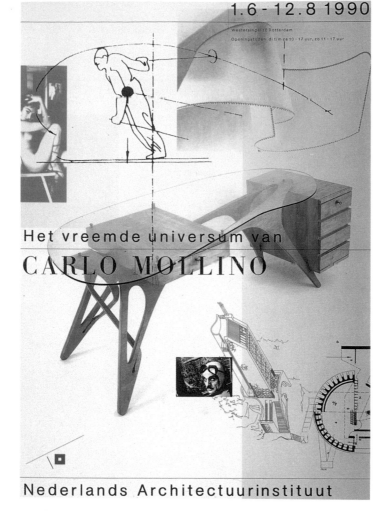

Poster ポスター

Carlo Mollino (Typografie Hollandaise Catalogue) The Netherlands 1991

AD,D:Henrik Barends   I:Mart Warmerdaw

DF:Studio Henrikbarends   CL:Design a la'maison du liver, do l'image et Du Son, Lyon

Poster ポスター

Boomtown Amsterdam (Typographie Hollandaise Catalogue) The Netherlands 1991

AD,D:Henrik Barends

I:Haico Beukers

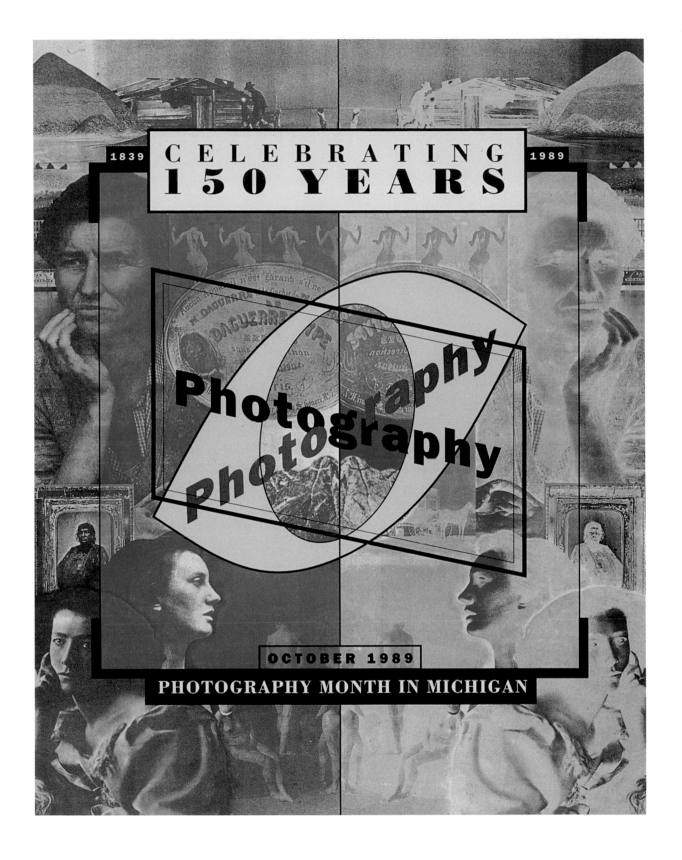

Poster ポスター

150 Years of Photography　USA 1989
AD.D:Katherine McCoy　P:Historic Photography
DF:McCoy & McCoy / Associates　CL:Detroit Institute of Arts

Poster ポスター

AIGA New Directions Poster 2 USA 1989
AD,D:Clifford Stoltze, Terry Swack P:Larry Joubert
DF:Clifford Stoltze Design, Terry Swack Design CL:AIGA Boston

Poster ポスター

AIGA New Directions Poster I　USA 1989

AD,D:Rick Stermole　AD,D:Clifford Stoltze

P:Stuart Darsh　DF:Clifford Stoltze Design　CL:AIGA Boston

Book Cover ブックカバー

Lettering by Design　UK 1992

D:Leonard Currie　DF:Leonard Currie Design

CL:Phaidon Press

Poster ポスター

April in April USA 199

AD.,D.:James A. Houff P:Paul Price

DF:James A. Houff C.:AIGA, Detroit Chapter

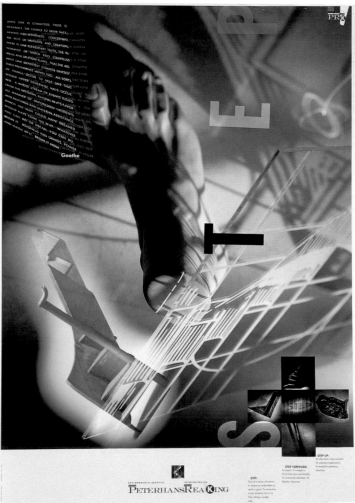

Poster ポスター

Step USA 1991

AD.,D.:James A. Houff P:Paul Price

DF:James A. Houff Design CL:Peterhans Rea

Poster ポスター

Communication Graphics   USA 1990
AD,D:James A.Houff   P:Paul Price
DF:James A.Houff   CL:AIGA Detroit Chapter

Posters ポスター

Men of Letters USA 1991
AD,D:Craig Frazier AD,P:John Casado
DF:Frazier Design CL:Display Lettering + Copy

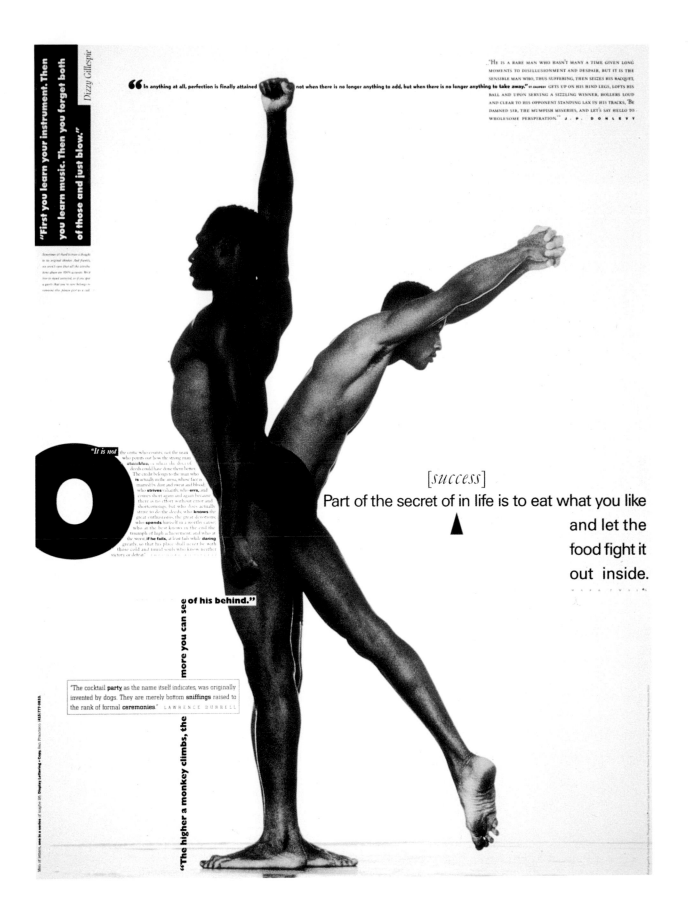

"In anything at all, perfection is finally attained not when there is no longer anything to add, but when there is no longer anything **to take away.**" SAINT EXUPÉRY

"HE IS A RARE MAN WHO HASN'T MANY A TIME GIVEN LONG MOMENTS TO DISILLUSIONMENT AND DESPAIR, BUT IT IS THE SENSIBLE MAN WHO, THUS SUFFERING, THEN SEIZES HIS RACQUET, BALL AND UPON SERVING A SIZZLING WINNER, HOLLERS LOUD AND CLEAR TO HIS OPPONENT STANDING LAX IN HIS TRACKS, 'BE DAMNED SIR, THE MUMPISH MISERIES, AND LET'S SAY HELLO TO WHOLESOME PERSPIRATION.'" J. P. DONLEVY

"It is not the critic who counts, not the man who points out how the strong man **stumbles,** or where the doer of deeds could have done them better. The credit belongs to the man who **is** actually in the arena, whose face is marred by dust and sweat and blood; who **strives** valiantly, who **errs,** and comes short again and again because there is no effort without error and shortcomings; but who does actually strive to do the deeds; who **knows** the great enthusiasms, the great devotions; who **spends** himself in a worthy cause; who at the best knows in the end the triumph of high achievement, and who at the worst, **if he fails,** at least fails while **daring** greatly, so that his place shall never be with those cold and timid souls who know neither victory or defeat." THEODORE ROOSEVELT

of his behind."

more you can see

"The cocktail **party,** as the name itself indicates, was originally invented by dogs. They are merely bottom **sniffings** raised to the rank of formal **ceremonies.**" LAWRENCE DURRELL

"The higher a monkey climbs, the

[*success*]

Part of the secret of in life is to eat what you like and let the food fight it out inside.

MARK TWAIN

Poster ポスター

Typocraft USA 1988

AD.D:James A. Houff P:Nancy Green

DF:James A. Houff CL:The Typocraft

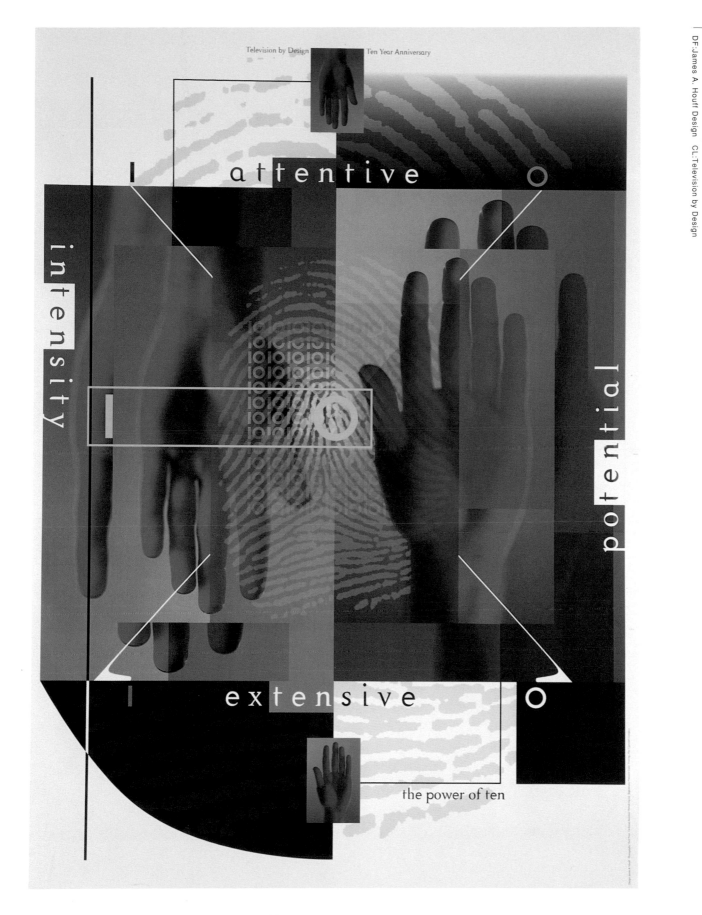

Poster ポスター

The Power of Ten USA 1993
CD:Melanie Goux AD,D,I:James A. Houff P:Paul Price
DF:James A. Houff Design CL:Television by Design

Invitation Card インビテーション・カード

Zeit-Reise (Time-Journe-) Switzerland 1993

AD,D:Cornel Windlin   P:Istvan Balogh

DF:Cornel Windlin   CL:Museum of Art and Design, Zurich

Brochure Spread ブロージュスページ

Detroit Artists Market Calendar Page [July] USA 1991

D:Brenda Rotheiser DF:Cranbrook Academy of Art, Department of Design

CL:Detroit Artists Market

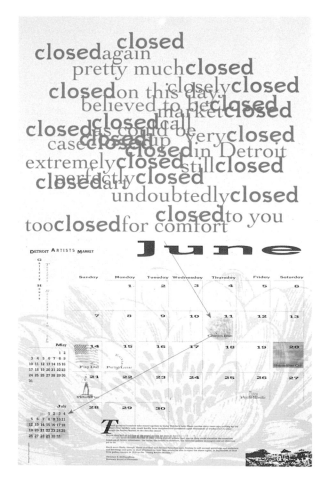

Postcard ポストカード

Grad Reception USA 1992

AD:Rebeca Mendez D:Darren Nemaye

DF:Art Center College of Design, Design Office CL:Art Center College of Design

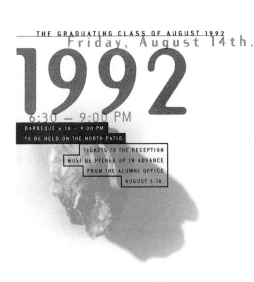

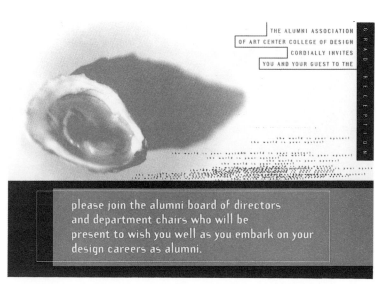

Invitation Card インビテーション・カード

Degree Show USA 1991

D:Brenda Rctheiser CF:Cranbrook Academy of Art, Department of Design

CL:Cranbrock Museum of Art

Poster ポスター

Harmony USA 1991

AD,D:James A. Houff P:Michelle Andonian

DF:James A. Houff Design CL:Television by Design

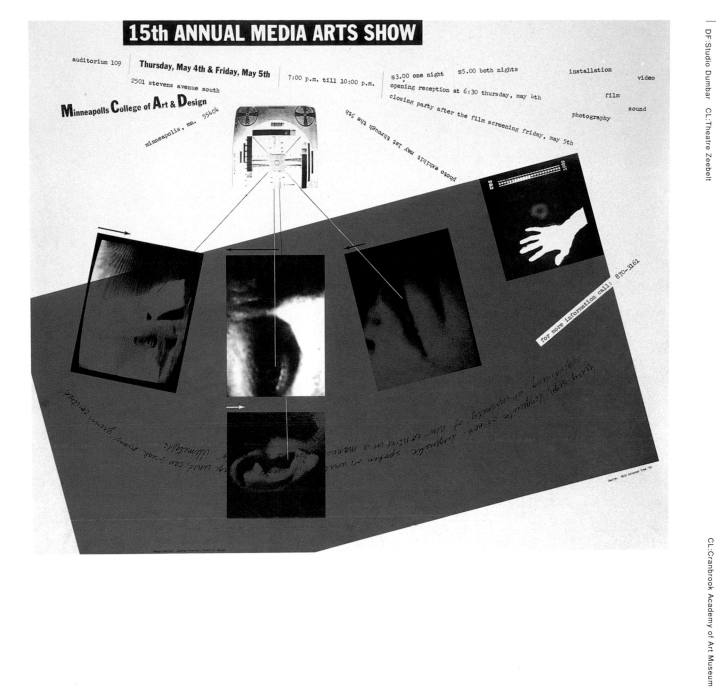

Poster ポスター

Theatre Zeebelt Affiche　USA 1991

AD:Gert Dumbar　D:Timorse　P:Lex Van Pieterson

DF:Studio Dumbar　CL:Theatre Zeebelt

Announcement Card アナウンスメント・カード

Do Not Think About The Blue Door　USA 1993

D.P:Brian Smith　DF:Cranbrook Academy of Art, Department of Design

CL:Cranbrook Academy of Art Museum

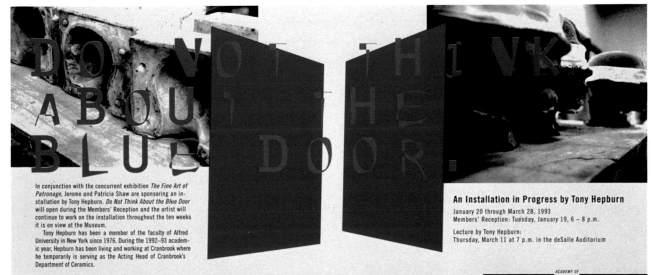

Poster ポスター
Murder as Phenomena USA 1992
AD,D:Raul Cabra
DF:Cabra Diseño CL San Francisco Camerawork

Poster ポスター
No Regular Joe USA 1992
AD.,D.:James A. Houff P.:FPG Photo
DF.:James A. Houff CL.:AIGA, Detroit Chapter

Brochure Cover ブローシュアカバー
Media Studies USA 1992
AD.:Carolyn Lamont D.,I.:James A. Houff P.:Mark Stern
DF.:James A. Houff Design CL.:The New School for Social Research

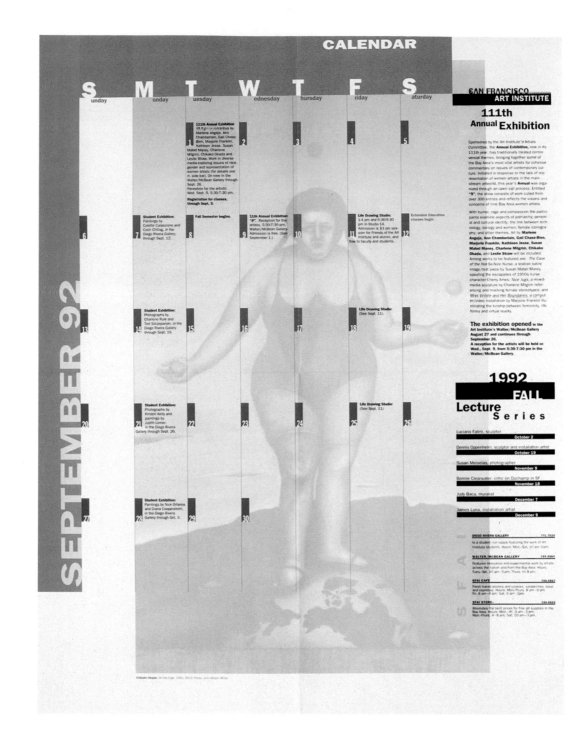

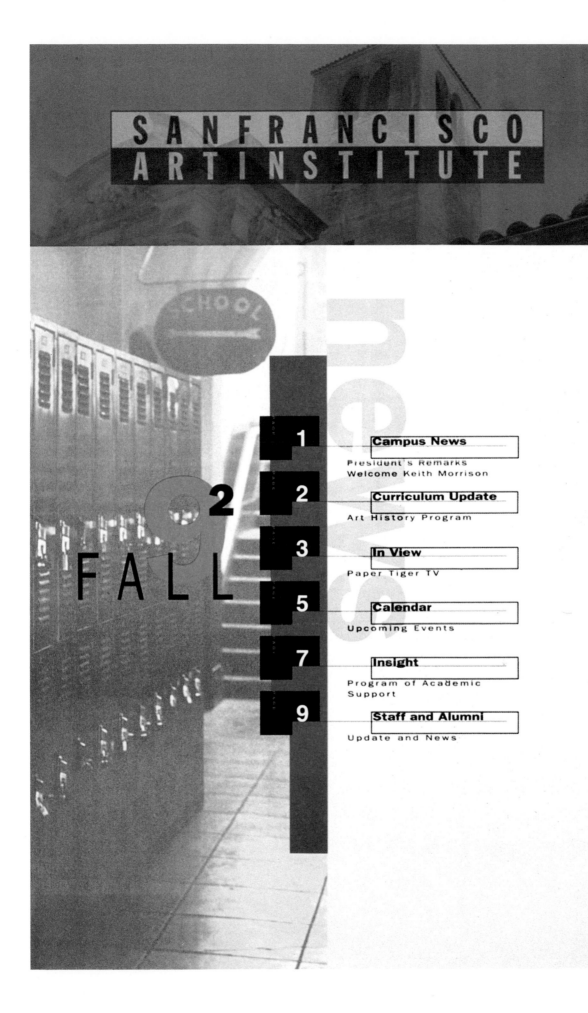

SANFRANCISCO ARTINSTITUTE

news

92 FALL

Poster ポスター

Saturday High USA 1992

AD:Rebeca Mendez C:Darin Beaman

DF:Art Center College of Design, Design Office CL:Art Center College of Design

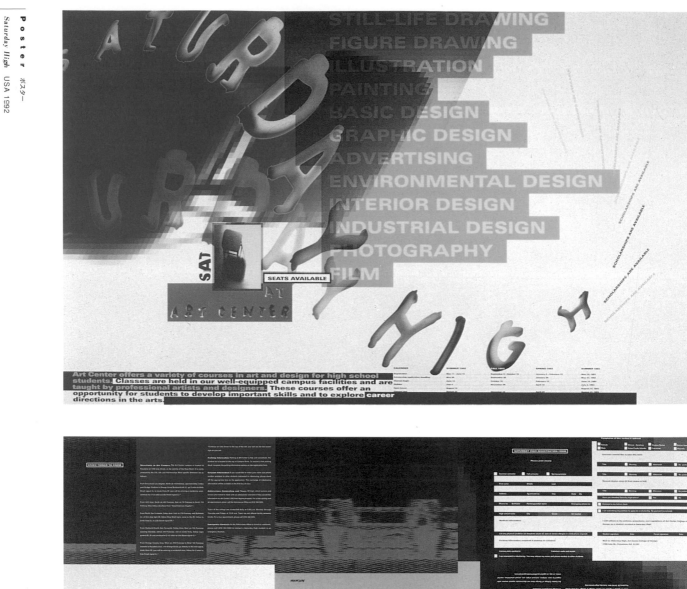

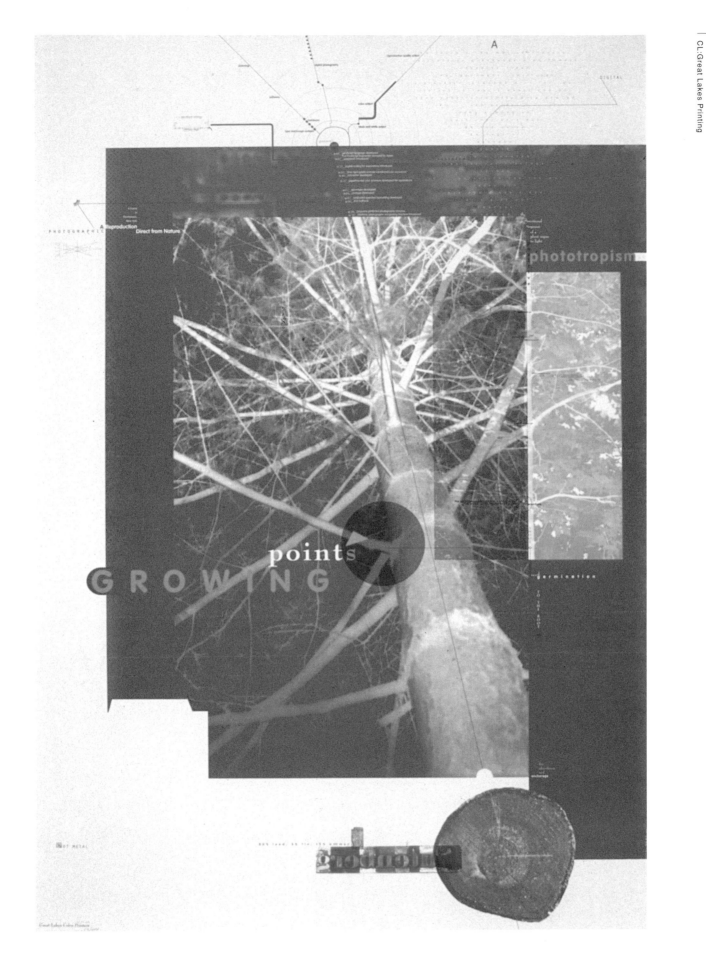

Poster ポスター

Growing Points USA 1992
D:Lisa Taft DF:Cranbrook Academy of Art, Department of Design
CL:Great Lakes Printing

Poster ポスター

Raising The Roof USA 1992

AD,D:Clifford Stoltze D:Timothy Smith

D,P:Rebecca Fagan

DF:Clifford Stoltze Design CL:Public Facilities Dept., City of Boston

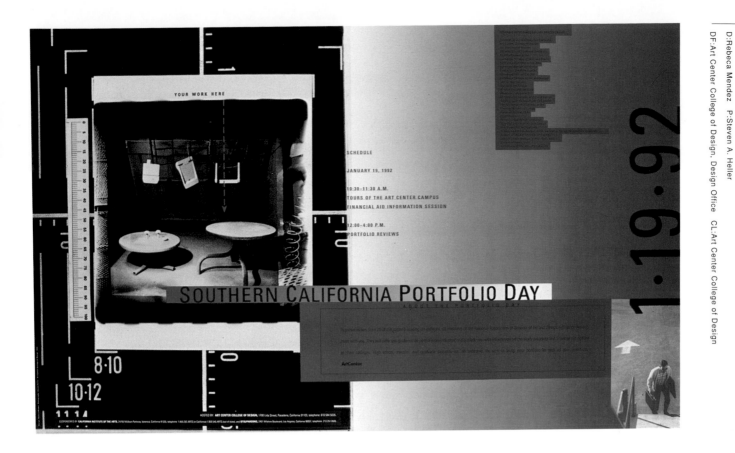

P o s t e r ポスター

Portfolio Day USA 1992

D:Rebeca Mendez P:Steven A. Heller

DF:Art Center College of Design, Design Office CL:Art Center College of Design

Poster ポスター

Tegentonen 1989 The Netherlands 1989

AD,D,I:Max Kisman D:Max Kisman

CL:Paradiso Amsterdam

Poster ポスター

Trap 5 The Netherlands 1991

AD,D:Koeweiden/Postma P:YANi

DF:Koeweiden/Postma CL:Frascati

Poster ポスター

Media Arts Announcement USA 1989
AD,D:Jan Jancourt D:Maria Alliconte, Donna Daubendiek, Kurt Lipisch, Timorse, Jutta Solberg
P:Stephen Pederson, Kirsti M.Hougen DF:MCAD Advanced Type '89 CL:Minneapolis College of Art & Design

Calendar カレンダー

Energy The Netherlands 1991
AD,D:Koeweiden/Postma P:YANi
DF:Koeweiden/Postma CL:Ministry of Economic Affairs

Poster ポスター
Saiten Klänge UK 1991
AD,D:Simon Staines
DF:Neville Brody Studios CL:Haus Der Kulturen Der Welt

Poster ポスター
Blas Musik UK 1990
AD,D:Simon Staines
DF:Neville Brody Studios CL:Haus Der Kulturen Der Welt

Magazine Spreads 雑誌ページ

"Output" USA 1992
D:Brian Smith, Richard Bates, David Shields, Susanna Stief
DF:Cranbrook Aceacemy of Art, Department of Design   CL:Student Project

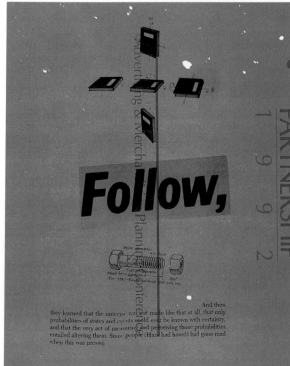

Posters ポスター
How Can I Show You Devotion USA 1992
D.P:Martin Venezky   D=:Cranbrook Academy of Art, Department of Design
CL:Student Project

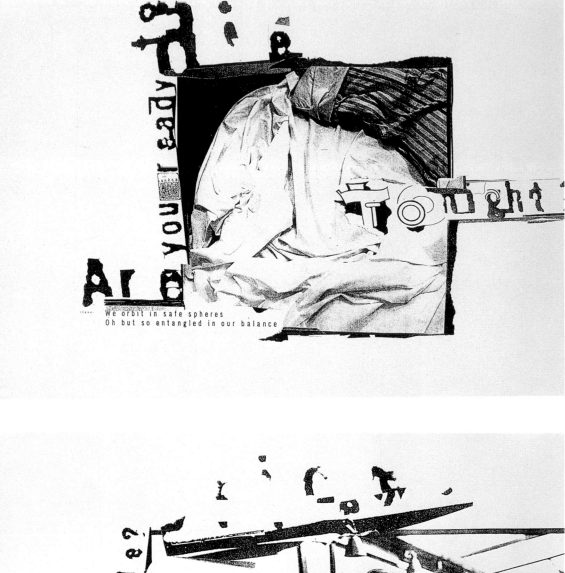

protess

Pure direction is about

never GETTING

where
you're GOING

installation
opens Jan 7th
and is open
24 hours
through May
7th

You're always MOVING

INDIVIDUATION

Announcement Card アナウンスメント・カード

Pure Direction USA 1992

D:Fred Bower DF:Cranbrook Academy of Art, Department of Design

CL:Self-Published _imited Edition

Magazine Spread 雑誌ページ

Stand by Your Man USA 1992

AD:David Carson D:P:Martin Venezky

DF:Cranbrook Academy of Art, Department of Design CL:Raygun Magazine

Poster ポスター

Keedy Typography USA 1991

D:Joan Dobbin DF:Cranbrook Academy of Art, Department of Design

CL:Student Project

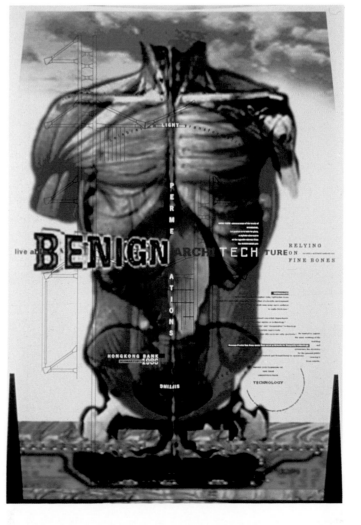

Poster ポスター

ACD 100 Show Call for Entries USA 1991
CD:Rob Dewey AD:Katherine McCoy D:Timothy O'Keeffe
DF:Cranbrook Academy of Art, Department of Design CL:American Center for Design

Poster ポスター

Benign Architecture USA 1992
CD:Katherine McCoy D:Mark Sylvester
DF:Cranbrook Academy of Art, Department of Design CL:Student Project

Poster ポスター

Capitalism W II Eat Itself" Switzerland 1992

AD,D:Cornel Windlin   DF:Cornel Windlin

CL:Fontshop International /Fuse Magazine

P o s t e r ポスター

Strafe für Rebellion-Vögel Switzerland 1990

AD,D,I:Cornel Windlin DF:Neville Brody Studio

CL:Touch Records

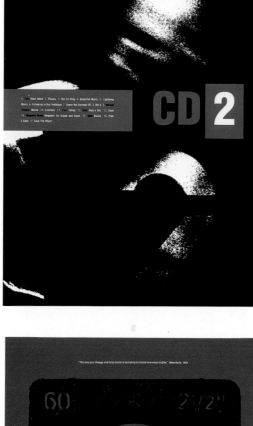

CD Packaging CDパッケージ

Z'ev - "One Fowl in The Grave" UK 1991

AD,D:Simon Staines D＝:Neville Brody Studios

CL:Touch

Announcement Card アナウンスメント・カード

Slightly Torqued USA 1992

D,P:Brian Smith DF:Cranbrook Academy of Art, Department of Design

CL:Cranbrook Academy of Art Museum

Two Decades of Photography by Carl Toth

This year Carl Toth celebrates his 20th anniversary as the founding Artist-in-Residence of the Academy's Department of Photography.

Slightly Torqued

MOST PHOTOGRAPHY DEPENDS ON BEING IMMEDIATELY RECOGNIZABLE. TO ME THINGS GET MORE INTERESTING WHEN YOU'RE NOT SURE WHAT SOMETHING REPRESENTS OR EVEN HOW IT WAS MADE. THERE MAY BE A DEGREE OF RECOGNIZABILITY BUT EVERYTHING SEEMS SLIGHTLY TORQUED.

September 30, 1992 through January 10, 1993
Members' Reception: Tuesday, September 29, 6 to 8 p.m.
Exhibition closed for Guy Fawkes Ball: November 2 through 13
Supported in part by the Michigan Council for Arts and Cultural Affairs.
500 Lone Pine Road, Bloomfield Hills, Michigan 48303-0801 (313) 645-3323

ACADEMY of
CRANBROOK ART MUSEUM

B o o k 本

"Das Geheul" by Allen Ginsberg Germany 1991

D:Lars Ohlerich

DF:Ohlerich Design

Record Cover レコードカバー

People Get Ready UK 1992

AD:Rob O'Connor

D:Chris Thomson P:Simon Fowler, Peter Calvin

BE MY FRIEND

PEOPLE GET READY

No. 2234

OCT 09 '91 16:28 MA

Record Cover レコードカバー

Blur UK 1992
AD：Rob O'Connor　D：Chris Thomson
P：David Grewcock　CL：Food Records

CD Packaging, Booklet CDパッケージ、ブックレット

Ryuichi Sakamoto -"Heart Beat" USA 1991-1992

AD.,D:Robert Bergman-Ungar P:Michel Comte

DF:Robert Bergman-Ungar/Art Direction CL:Virgin Japan

CD Packaging CDパッケージ

Ryuichi Sakamoto -"You Do Me" USA 1991-1992

AD.D:Robert Bergman-Ungar P:Albert Watson

DF:Robert Bergman-Ungar/Art Direction CL:Virgin Japan

Record, CD, Cassette Packaging レコード, CD, カセットパッケージ

Ryuichi Sakamoto -"Beuty" USA 1991-1992

AD.D:Robert Bergman-Ungar P:Albert Watson

DF:Robert Bergman-Ungar/Art Direction CL:Virgin Japan

Greeting Card グリーティング・カード

Hi-Hat Studio Japan 1992

AD,D,P:Isamu Nakazawa DF:Hi-Hat Studio

CL:Hi-Hat Studio

Record Packaging レコードパッケージ

Dominadea Switzerland 1991

AD,D,P,I:Hans-Rudolf DF:Lutz

CL:Unknownmix

Record and CD Packaging レコード・CDパッケージ

Papa Sprain - May JK 1992

AD,DI:Paul Khera D,I:Maria Beddoes

DF:Paul Khera CL:H.Ark!

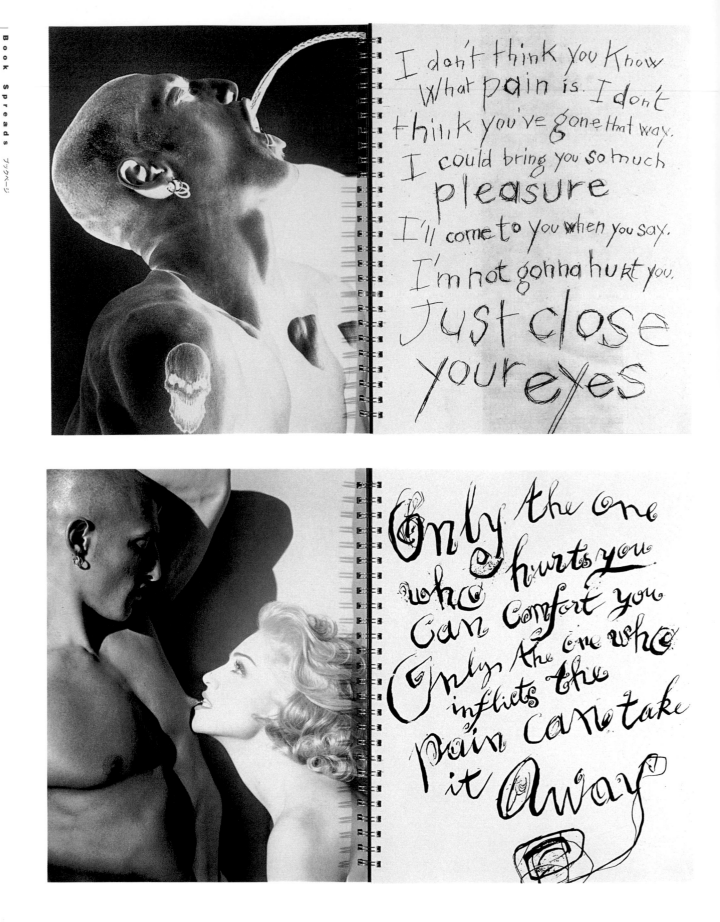

Book Spreads ブックページ

Madonna - "Sex"   USA 1392

CD:Fabien Baron   D:Siung Fat Tjia, Patrick Li, Steve Jacobsen
P:Steven Meisel   CL:Madonna Sex Book

Poster ポスター

Grass Men's Japan 1992
AD,D:Koichi Yoshida   P:Nicci Keller
CL:Grass International

Advertising Spread 広告ページ

Issey Miyake Stretch USA 1991
CD:Fabien Baron   P:Tyen
CL:Issey Miyake

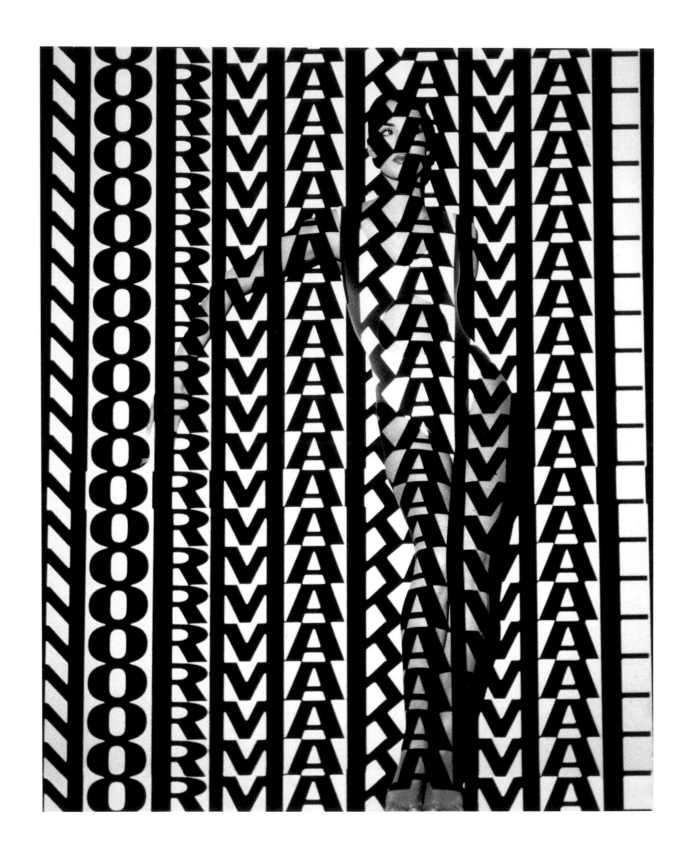

Advertisement 広告物

Norma Kamali Advertising Campaign USA 1991

CD:Fabien Baron P:Steven Meisel

CL:Norma Kamali

NORMA KAMALI

PRODUZIONE ZAMASPORT.MILANO.VIA DELLA SPIGA,49.TEL.782.182.SORDEVOLO.LIGHT PARIS LILY ST.TROPEZ.MEREDITH PARIS

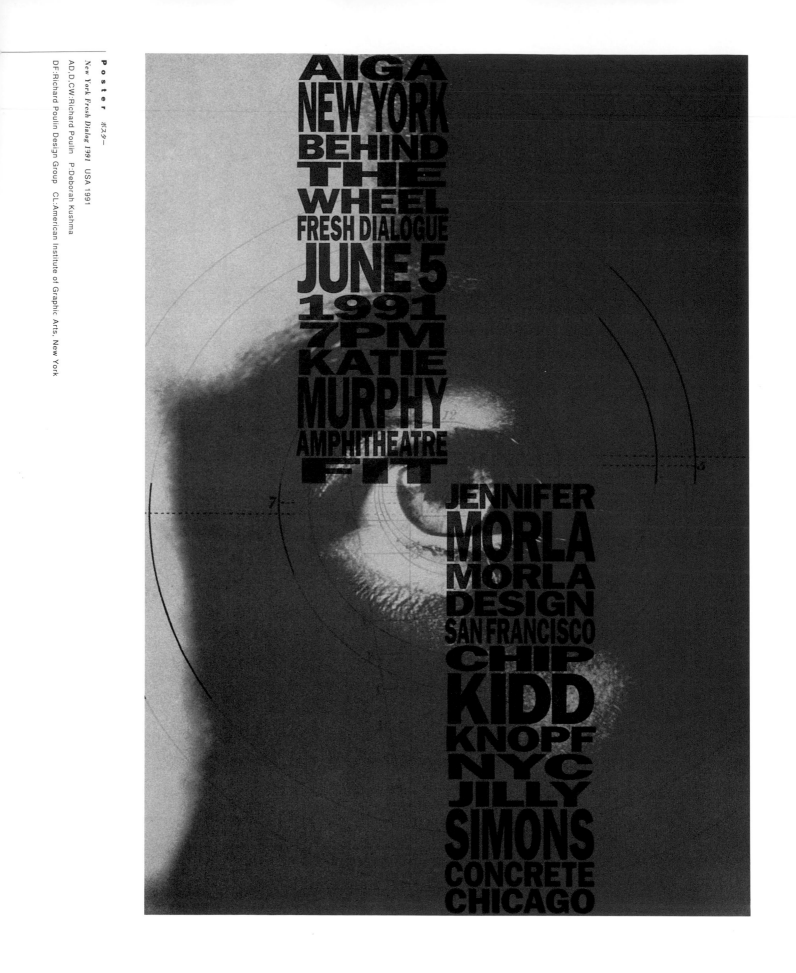

Poster ポスター
New York Fresh Dialog 1991 USA 1991
AD,D,CW:Richard Poulin P:Deborah Kushma
DF:Richard Poulin Design Group CL:American Institute of Graphic Arts, New York

98 Discovery August 1992   Discovery August 1992 99

Magazine Spread 雑誌ページ

Learning to Smile Hong Kong 1992

AD,D:Andrea Koura, Percy Chung CW:Ron Gluckman

DF:Emphasis (Hong Kong) CL:Cathay Pacific Airways

Advertisement 広告物

Bags USA

CD:Jef Loeb, Caulton Taylor AD,D:Cabell Ellington P:Fred Vauderpoel

TY:Andresen DF:Katsin/Loeb Advertiging CL:Stonaridge

Magazine 誌

"*Bazaar*" *Sep '92* USA 1992

CD:Fabien Baron AD:Joel Berg

P:Patrick Demarchelier, Peter Lindbergh CL:Bazaar

remember a time

when genders

were bent, rules

broken, inhibitions

shed, and all the

best girls were

pretty wild?

Magazine Spread 雑誌ページ

"Bazaar" Jan '93 USA 1993
CD:Fabien Baron AD:Joel Berg
P.:Patrick Demarcheller CL:Bazaar

FROM LEFT: SILK DRESS, ABOUT $650, AND LEGGINGS; MIDRIFF, SHIRT, PEAR-PRINT DRESS, ABOUT $985, AND CAPRIS. ALL, MARC JACOBS FOR PERRY ELLIS.

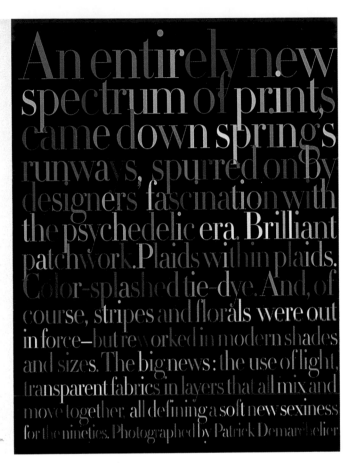

An entirely new spectrum of prints, came down spring's runways, spurred on by designers' fascination with the psychedelic era. Brilliant patchwork. Plaids within plaids. Color-splashed tie-dye. And, of course, stripes and florals were out in force—but reworked in modern shades and sizes. The big news: the use of light, transparent fabrics in layers that all mix and move together, all defining a soft new sexiness for the nineties. Photographed by Patrick Demarchelier

Magazine Spreads 雑誌ページ

"Bazaar" Sep '92 USA 1992
CD:Fabien Baron AD:Joel Berg
P:Patrick Demarchelier; Peter Lindbergh CL:Bazaar

B L A C K
leather

Motorcycle mania brought black leather as much into the fashion vernacular as the little black dress. While the trend made us more comfortable wearing what had always been considered the outward manifestation of a dangerous mind, the fascination quickly degenerated when a flock of Perfecto-wearing poseurs turned the biker jacket into something so routine, so overworked, that all its original seduction and rebellion were lost. This fall, designers rescue black leather from the tired Hell's Angels idiom. It shows up everywhere with a chic new edge, in forms that are wearable, diverse, and anything but commonplace. Quilted pants. Sculpted jackets. Long slit skirts banded with white. What's also different is that these new pieces are not confined to one look, or one context: Now leather pants work in the office, worn with a white shirt. Black leather still gives a feeling of protection, of invincibility, but its connotations have changed from sinister to sexy. In times like these, it can't hurt to don a literal thick skin. The new artistry in black leather. Opposite page: Fitted jacket, about $3285, quilted pants, about $3035, and combat boots, about $1045, all by Karl Lagerfeld for Chanel.

Q
fall's refined appeal

uiet luxury, considered line, beautiful fabrics: These are the qualities that epitomize the new elegance that underlies fall's flashier changes. These are clothes beyond the seasonal vagaries of fashion, yet within their timeless appeal show real, substantive changes that are absolutely of the moment. A sweeping black evening dress that bares only the shoulders in a statement of subtle exposure. A soft gray coatdress worn with matching trousers, in a completely original variation on the suit. "Elegance is understatement," says Calvin Klein. "The woman should stand out; the clothes should not overtake her." There's an integrity of design that allows these pieces to stand on their own: They don't need the glittery camouflage of a wristful of bracelets or strands of necklaces to look finished. "That ethic of jeweled, fussy, scalloped, and teased is just not in my world anymore," says Isaac Mizrahi. "Now a scent, a defined eyebrow, is all you need." Impeccable in balance, cut, and proportion, these are the clothes that, by virtue of their practicality, their lack of pretension, are the foundation of a great wardrobe. A new grace comes to evening. Opposite page: Black viscose/Lycra turtleneck, drop-waist dress, about $1375, by Donna Karan.

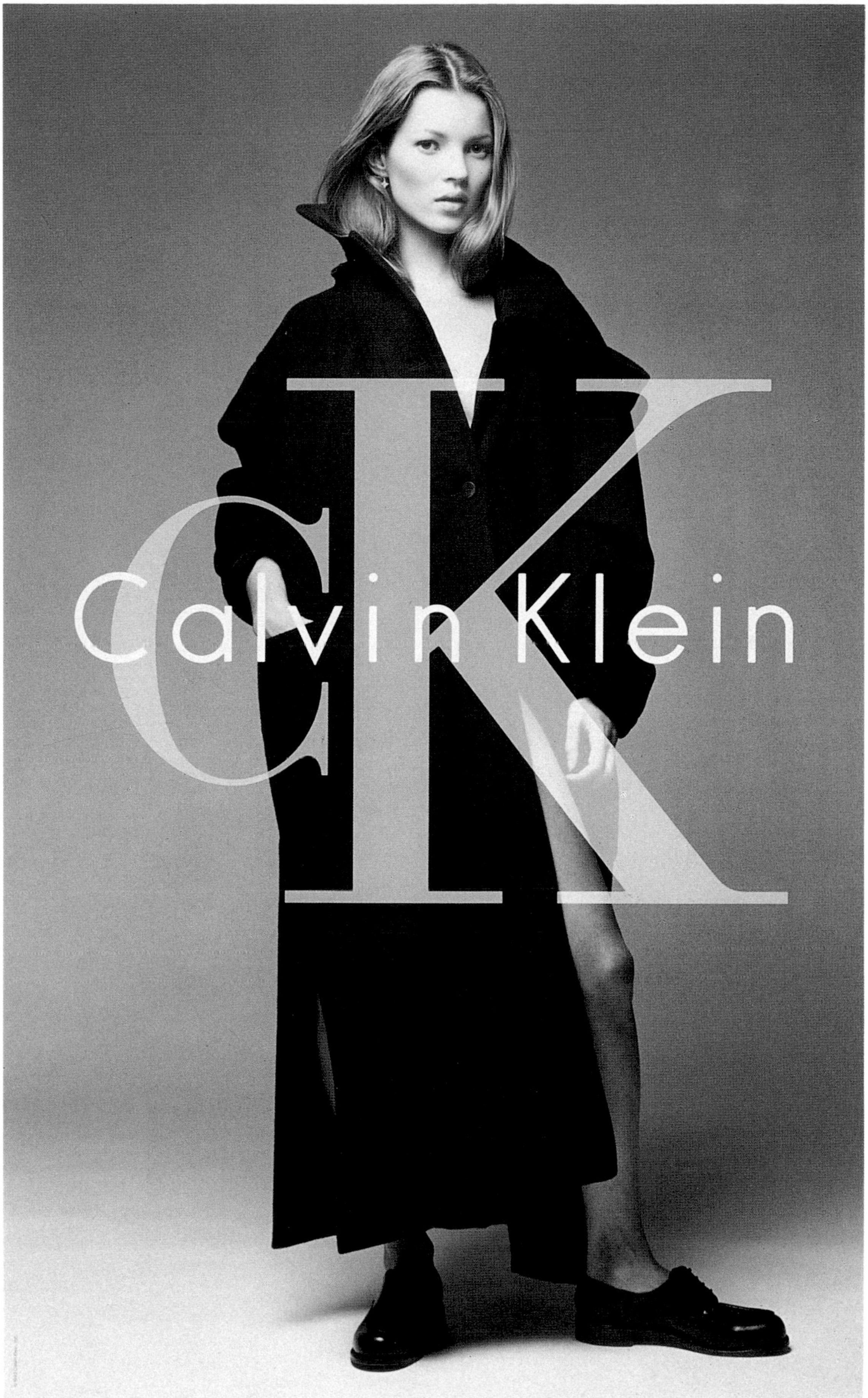

Advertisement 広告物

CK Calvin Klein USA 1993

CD:Neil Kraft AD:Madonna Johnson

P:Patrick Demarchelier CL:CK Calvin Klein

Poster ポスター

Abahouse Image   Japan 1991
AD,D:Malcolm Garret   Artist Agency:C.W.C.
CL:Abahouse International

Magazine Advertisement 雑誌広告

Abahouse Devinette   Japan 1992
AD,D:Patrick Glover   I:Junko Sakuraba
Artist Agency:C.W.C.   CL:Abahouse International

Book Spread ブックページ
Collaboration Japan 1990
AD:Keizo Matui D:Yuko Araki
P:Seiichi Tanaka CL:Seiichi Tanaka

Catalogue Spread カタログページ
Abahouse Handbook Japan 1992
AD,D:Hitoshi Nakamura (Keen's) P:François Deconinck
CL:Abahouse International

Brochure Spread ブローシュアスペッジ

WJNK USA 1992

CD:Joel Fuller AD.D:Tom Sterling P:Gallen Mei

DF:Pinkhaus Design CL:WJMK

Brochure ブローシュア

Eric Meola by Rex USA 1990

CD:Joel Fuller AD.D:Mark Cantor P:Eric Meola

DF:Pinkhaus Design CL:Steve Miller, Rex Three

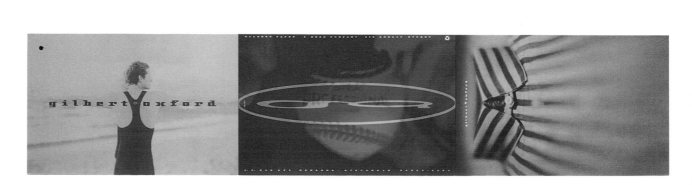

Book Cover ブックカバー

Oxford Chipbook USA 1990

CD:Joel Fuller AD.D:Mark Cantor P:Gallen Mei

DF:Pinkhaus Design CL:Su McGlouchlin, Gilbert Paper

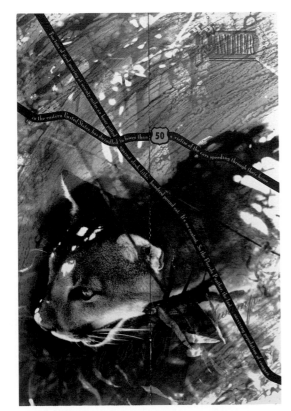

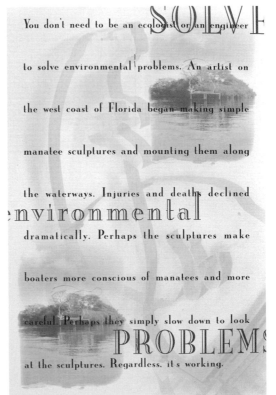

Brochure Spreads　ブロ－シュアスペ－ジ

What Is Smart　USA 1990

CD,AD,D:Joel Fuller　AD:Mark Cantor　AD,D:Tom Sterling

DF:Pinkhaus Design　CL:Gilbert Paper

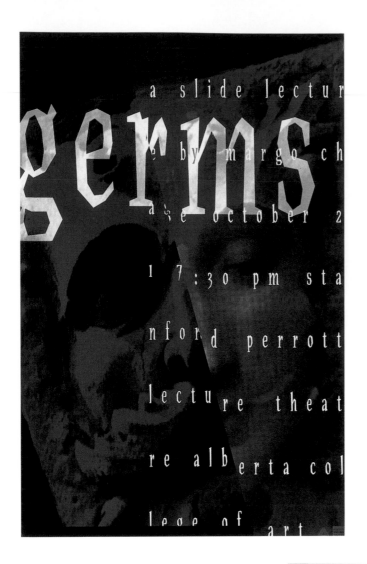

Poster ポスター

Germs USA 1991

AD,D:Margo Chase   DF:Margo Chase Design

CL:Alberta College of Arts

Poster ポスター

Campaign for Internal Stock Voting   USA 1992

AD:Nancy Paynter   D:Raul Cabra

P:Marilyn Hulbert   DF:Cabra Diseño   CL:Chevron

Musique et Danse

octobre en normandie
du 1er au 31 octobre 1991

Rouen. Hangar 23
Port autonome
Bd. Émile Duchemin
France

locations:
Rouen: 35 70 04 07
Le Havre: 35 21 41 21
Dieppe: 35 82 04 43

le Conseil Général de la Seine-Maritime finance octobre en normandie

Poster ポスター
"Festival Octobre en Normandie" 1991   France 1991
AD.D:Philippe Apeloig
CL:Dance and Music Festival: "Octobre en normandie"

musique et danse

octobre en normandie
1er - 31 octobre 1992

locations:
Rouen: 35 70 04 07
Le Havre: 35 21 41 21
Dieppe: 35 82 04 43

Poster ポスター
1992 season of the "Festival Octobre en Normandie".   France 1992
AD.D:Philippe Apeloig
CL:Dance and Music Festival: "Octobre en normandie"

Poster ポスター

Cargo Canada 1991

AD,D:Lumbago   D:Sylvain Racine

P:Michel Pilon   DF:Lumbago   CL:Prima Films

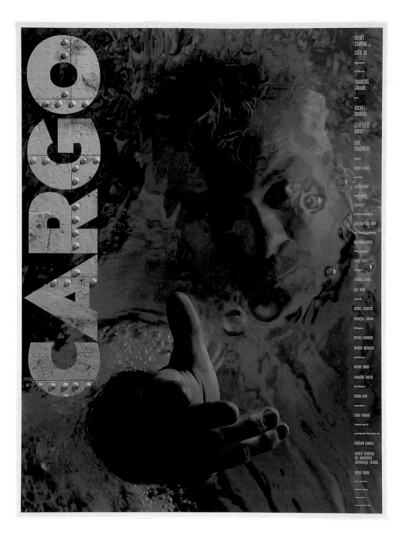

Poster ポスター

Pirandello   The Netherlands 1990

AD,D:Koeweiden/Postma   DF:Koeweiden/Postma

CL:Theatre Frascati

3 avril-24 juillet 1992

Didier Imbert
19 avenue Matignon
Paris

MOORE

HENRY MOORE INTIME

collection de l'artiste

Poster ポスター
Henry Moore Exhibition "Intime" at Galerie Didier Imbert, Paris, 1992. France 1992
AD,D:Philippe Apeloig
CL:Didier Imbert Fine Art

Poster ポスター

The Kill-Off USA 1990

AD:Jennifer Schumacher   AD.P.CW:Thomas Starr   D:Jennifer Washburn

P:Thomas Starr   DF:Thomas Starr & Associates   CL:Cabriolet Films

Poster ポスター

Jerzy Kosinski - The Face and Masks   Poland 1992
AD.D.CW:Tadeusz Piechura   P:Czesław Czapliński
DF:Atelier Tadeusz Piechura   CL:Museum of Art, Lodzi

Poster ポスター

"Centre National de Danse Contemporaine d'Angers l'Esquisse, 1992". France 1992
AD.D:Philippe Apeloig
CL:CNDC l'Esquisse

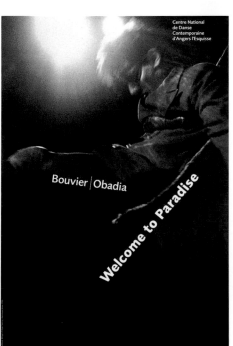

Envelope 封書

Ziffnet/Mac New Membership Kit   USA 1992

AD:Kathy Forsythe   D:Jane Cuthbertson   P:Ralph Mercer

DF:Forsythe Design   CL:Ziffnet

Poster ポスター

Alfred University   USA 1987

AD.D.P:Ramona Hutko   DF:Ramona Hutko Design

CL:Alfred University

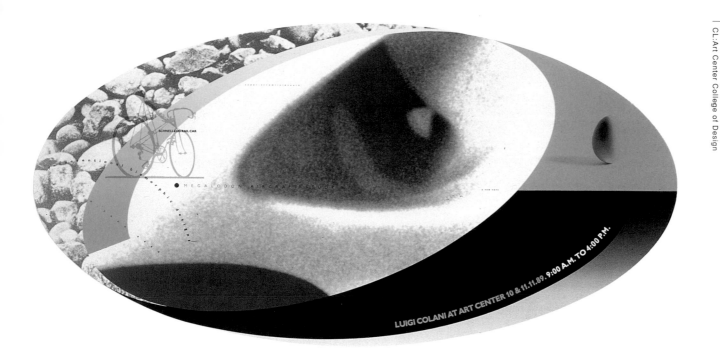

Poster ポスター

Luigi Colani USA 1989

D:Rebeca Mendez DF:Art Center College of Design, Design Office

CL:Art Center College of Design

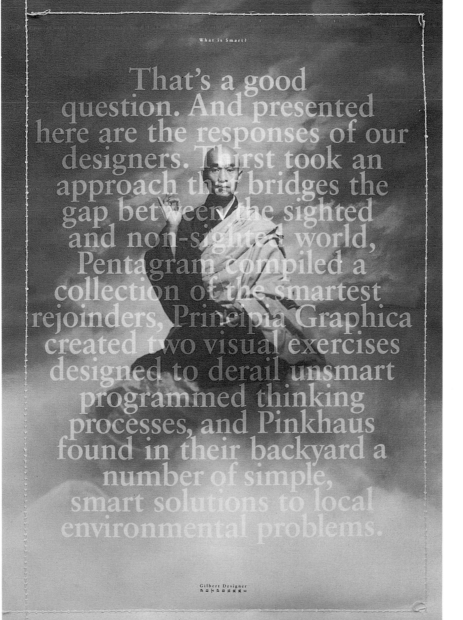

Packaging パッケージ

Designer Potpourri USA 1991

AD,D:Joel Fuller, Tom Sterling P:Michele Clement

DF:Pinkhaus Design CL:Su McGlouchlin, Gilbert Paper

Poster ポスター

Oklahoma Conference USA 1991

AD.D.I:John Muller P:Michael Regnier

DF:Muller + Co. CL:Muller + Co.

Poster ポスター

Biannual Show USA 1989

CD.D:Joel Fuller AD.D:Tom Sterling

DF:Pinkhaus Design CL:AIGA, Miami Chapter

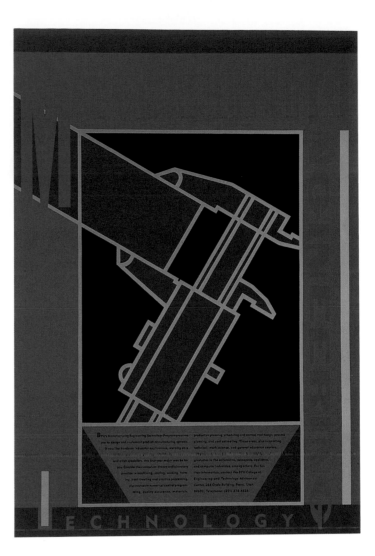

Poster ポスター

Manufacturing Engineering USA 1990

AD:Mac Magleby TY:Jonathan Skousen D,I:Lily McCullough

DF:BYU Graphics CL:Brigham Young University Engineering Dept

Poster ポスター

All-British Field Meet USA 1991

AD,D:Jack Anderson D:David Bates P:Dennis Howell

DF:Hornall Anderson Design Works CL:Puget Sound British Motoring Society

Calendar カレンダー

Calendar of Amsterdam A-chitecture The Netherlands 1988-1989

AD,D:Wim Verboven P:Tjeerd Frederikse

CW:Cilly Jansen DF:Tctal Design CL:Van Soest

Poster ポスター

Osaka Collection Poster I　Japan 1992
CD:Hiroshi Narasaki　AD,D:Masayuki Shimizu　D:Shingo Musoh
P:Katuzi Nisikawa　DF:Heter-O-Doxy Protprast　CL:Osaka Collection Organizing Committee

Poster ポスター

Onna no Shiro Japan 1989

AD,D:Keisuke Unosawa   I:Keiko Hirano

DF:Keisuke Unosawa Design   CL:Himeji City Museum of Art

Onna no shiro

女の城　1989年5月6日🈓 7日🈰　姫路市市民会館・姫路市総社 本町112番地
開場 10:00a.m. 入場料 300yen(但し,ホリ・ヒロシ公演,お茶席など一部別料金です)
開催イベント　ホリ・ヒロシ公演・シンポジューム「21世紀の女たちへ」・ファッションショー・グルメコーナー
展示「嫁ぐ日の夢・100年の対照」「花の競艶」・ファイナルコンサート(京都フィルハーモニー) その他多数
お問い合わせ・姫路100周年行事実行委員会 0792・84・0100

P o s t e r s ポスター

Alpha Cubic Japan 1991
CD:Junichi Morimoto AD.D:Yoshinari Hisazumi
P:Katsutoshi Hatsuzawa DF:Hakuhodo CL:Alpha Cubic

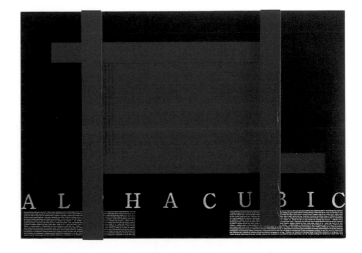

Poster ポスター

U - calendar page UK 1993

D:Phil Baines DF:Phil Baines

CL:Nord/lb, Commissioned by Meta Design, Berlin

084

Leftmost panel

Save the date!

Thursday
1 November
1990

Independent
Curators
Incorporated
15th
Anniversary
Celebration

Gala Benefit
Cocktails and
Dinner
Leo Castelli
Guest of Honor

Exhibition and
Silent Auction
Saturday
27 October
through
cocktails
Thursday
1 November

Second panel

Independent
Curators
Incorporated
15th
Anniversary
Benefit
Exhibition
and
Silent Auction

27 October
through
1 November
1990

Hosted by
Bess Cutler
Gallery
593 Broadway
(between Houston
and Prince Streets)

Over 150 works
in all media by
an international
group of
younger as well
as established
artists from ICI
exhibitions.

Checklist and
bid-by-mail
forms are
available.

Benefit Party
Thursday
1 November
Cocktails, Silent
Auction, Dinner

Viewing and
Bidding Hours

Saturday
27 October
10:00 – 6:00

Sunday
28 October
Noon – 6:00

Monday
29 October
10:00 – 6:00

Tuesday
30 October
10:00 – 6:00

Wednesday
31 October
10:00 – 6:00

Thursday
1 November
10:00 – 2:00

For more
information
please call
Mary LaVigne
at ICI
212.254.8200

ICI is a
non-profit
organization
dedicated
exclusively to
organizing and
circulating
traveling
exhibitions of
contemporary
art.

Main leaflet

Independent
Curators
Incorporated
Fifteenth
Anniversary
Celebration and
Gala Benefit

ICI's Board of Trustees and
Benefit Committees cordially
invite you to a Gala Benefit
Party, Exhibition and Silent
Auction in celebration of ICI's
Fifteenth Anniversary.

Leo Castelli, Guest of Honor

Inauguration of THE LEO,
a bi-annual ICI award to
an individual who has made an
outstanding contribution to
the international contemporary
art world.

Presentation of THE LEO
to John Russell.

Thursday, 1 November 1990

**Cocktail Party and
Silent Auction**
6:00 to 8:30 pm

Silent Auction of art donated
by more than 150 artists whose
work has been included in ICI's
recent exhibitions.

Hosted by
Bess Cutler Gallery
593 Broadway

Dinner and Entertainment
8:30 pm

The Columns
584 Broadway

Informal Dress

Benefit Exhibition and Silent Auction
The Exhibition and Silent Auction will be
open to the public for viewing and bidding
from Saturday, October 27 to Thursday,
November 1 when the bidding will end
at 8:30 pm.

**Artists Committee for the
Benefit Exhibition and Silent Auction**
All members of the Artists Committee as well
as over 125 other artists have contributed
works to the Silent Auction.

Christo, Co-Chairman
Dorothea Rockburne, Co-Chairman

Ida Applebroog
Tony Berlant
Bruno Ceccobelli
Helen Chadwick
Sue Coe
Gianni Dessì
Jean Fisher
Leon Golub
Hans Haacke
Sfida Ishani
Kristin Jones and Andrew Ginzel
Komar & Melamid
Frank Majore
Allan McCollum
Duane Michals
Anne & Patrick Poirier
Ray Smith
Elke Solomon
Nancy Spero
Gary Stephan
Juan Uslé
Meyer Vaisman
William Wegman
Fred Wilson

**Silent Auction
Viewing and Bidding Hours**

Day	Date	Hours
Saturday	October 27	10:00 – 6:00 pm
Sunday	October 28	10:00 – 6:00 pm
Monday	October 29	10:00 – 6:00 pm
Tuesday	October 30	10:00 – 6:00 pm
Wednesday	October 31	10:00 – 6:00 pm
Thursday	November 1	10:00 – 2:00 pm

Independent Curators Incorporated
is a national non-profit traveling
exhibition service dedicated exclusively
to contemporary art. Founded in 1975,
ICI organizes and circulates exhibitions
which are presented throughout the
United States and Canada, as well
as Europe and Mexico, to date, over 250
museums, university art galleries, art
centers and alternative spaces have
utilized ICI's exhibition services. ICI
exhibitions present a broad range
of recent developments and aesthetic
concerns internationally, and have
included the work of more than 1,000
well known and lesser known artists.
These exhibitions enable arts
institutions of all sizes to introduce their
audiences to a wider range of
contemporary art, and provide artists
with the opportunity-sometimes their
first-to exhibit their work nationally
and internationally. ICI's activities are
made possible, in part, by individual
contributions and grants from
foundations, corporations and the
National Endowment for the Arts.

Independent Curators Incorporated
799 Broadway, Suite 205
New York, NY 10003
212.254.8200

Catalogue カタログ

De La Photo De Mode Monaco　USA 1992

CD:Fabien Baron　Design Director:Siung Fal Tjia　Design Coordinator:Patrick Li

D:Baron & Baron Advertising　CL:Festival International

Quatrieme Festival International de la Photo de Mode Monaco 1992

QUATRIEME
FESTIVAL
INTERNATIONAL
DE LA PHOTO
DE MODE
MONACO 1992
SOUS LE HAUT
PATONAGE
DU MINISTERE
DE LA CULTURE
ET DE LA
COMMUNICATION

Invitation 招待状
Norma Kamali Invitation USA 1991
CD:Fabien Baron
CL:Norma Kamali

Invitation 招待状
Michael Kors Invitation USA 1991
CD:Fabien Baron
CL:Michael Kors

Direct Mails ダイレクトメール
Junmen Sale Campaigns Japan 1992
AD,D:Keisuke Unosawa
DF:Keisuke Unosawa CL:Jun

Catalogue カタログ

Typographie Hollandaise The Netherlands 1991

AD,D:Henrik Barends P:Paul De Nooijer

DF:Studio Henrikbarends CL:Design a la maison du livre, de l'image et Du Son, Lyon

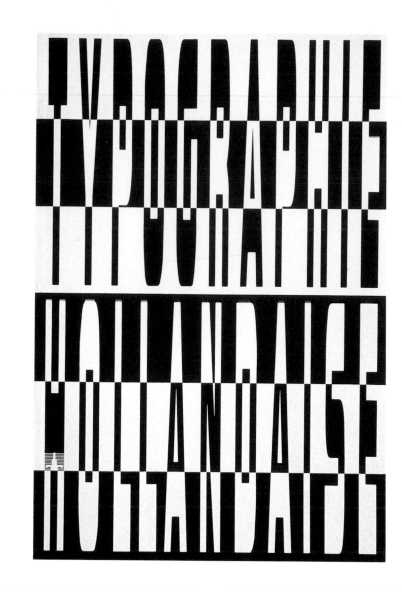

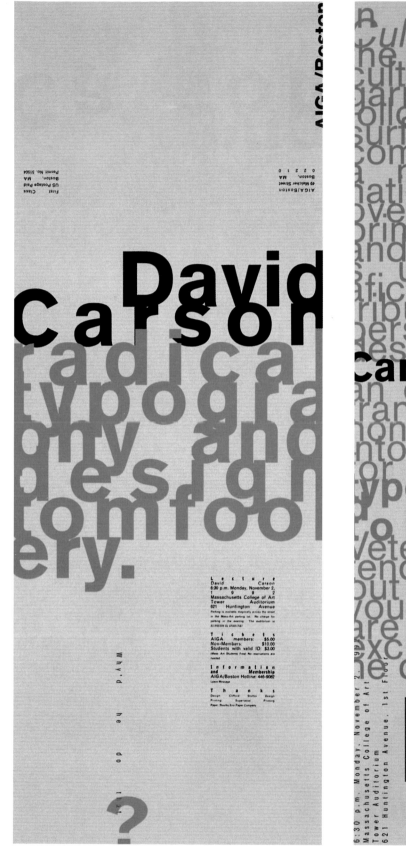

Leaflet リーフレット

David Carson Announcement USA 1992

CD,D:Clifford Stoltze DF:Clifford Stoltze Design

CL:AIGA

Postcard ポストカード
The Gift of Discovery USA 1992
AD,D,I:Carlos Segura
DF:Segura CL:Gimcracks

Postcard ポストカード
Markus Alkire Announcement Cards - Series of 3 USA 1993
D:Robert Beerman I:Markus Alkire
DF:Robert Beerman CL:Markus Alkire

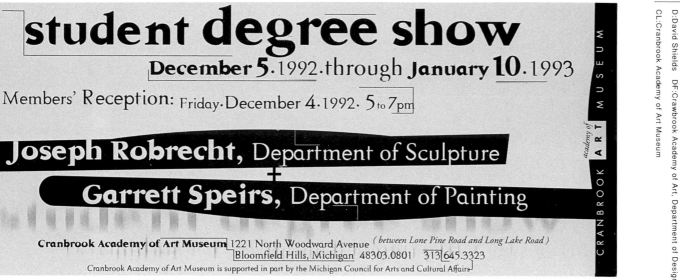

student degree show

December 5.1992.through January 10.1993

Members' Reception: Friday.December 4.1992. 5 to 7pm

Joseph Robrecht, Department of Sculpture
✝
Garrett Speirs, Department of Painting

Cranbrook Academy of Art Museum 1221 North Woodward Avenue *(between Lone Pine Road and Long Lake Road)*
Bloomfield Hills, Michigan 48303.0801 313 645.3323
Cranbrook Academy of Art Museum is supported in part by the Michigan Council for Arts and Cultural Affairs

CRANBROOK academy of ART MUSEUM

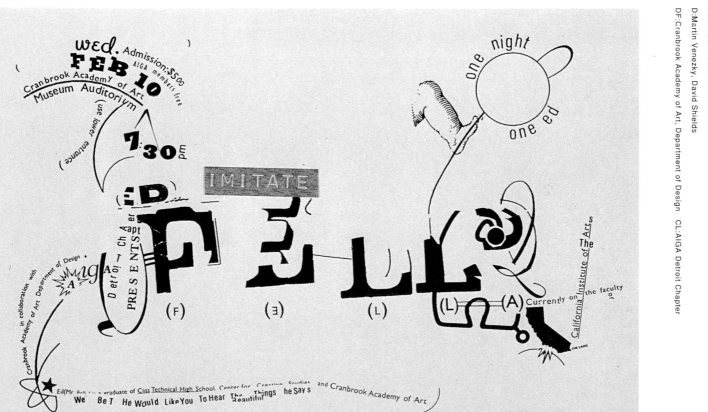

Announcement Card アナウンスメント・カード
Student Degree Show USA 1992
D:David Shields DF:Cranbrook Academy of Art, Department of Design
CL:Cranbrook Academy of Art Museum

Postcard ポストカード
Fella USA 1993
D:Martin Venezky, David Shields
DF:Cranbrook Academy of Art, Department of Design CL:AIGA Detroit Chapter

Signing サイン

New Alphabet for Parliament House Australia Australia 1988

CD:Garry Emery AD.D Emery Vincent Design

DF:Emery Vincent Design CL:Mitchell/Giurgola & Thorp

Record Cover レコードカバー

Brilliant Tapestry UK 1992

AD:Rob O'Connor D:Stuart Mackenzie

DF:Stylorouge CL:Virgin Records

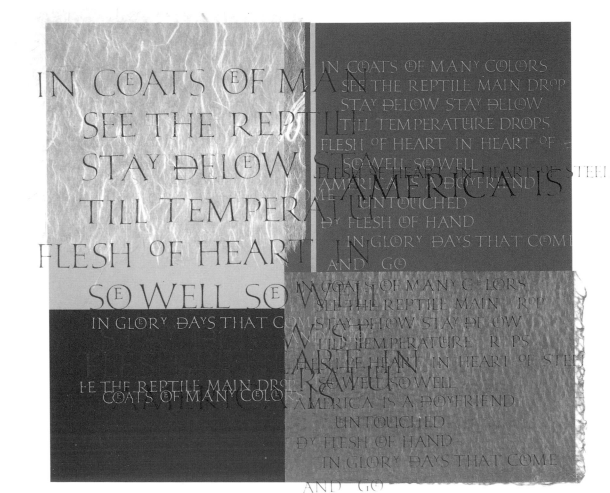

Catalogue Cover　カタログカバー

The Best Book Design 1991　The Netherlands 1992

D:Menno Landstra　DF:Stichting

CL:Stichting

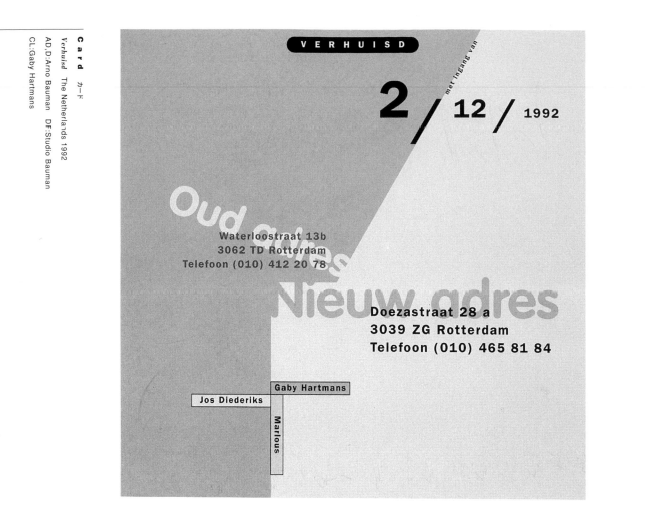

Card カード
Verhuisd The Netherlands 1992
AD,D:Arno Bauman DF:Studio Bauman
CL:Gaby Hartmans

VERHUISD

2 / 12 / 1992

met ingang van

Oud adres

Waterloostraat 13b
3062 TD Rotterdam
Telefoon (010) 412 20 78

Nieuw adres

Doezastraat 28 a
3039 ZG Rotterdam
Telefoon (010) 465 81 84

Gaby Hartmans

Jos Diederiks

Marlous

Brochure Cover ブローシュアカバー
Budget Dordrecht The Netherlands 1992
CD:Arno Bauman AD,D:Jan Pinto
DF:Studio Bauman CL:City of Dordrecht

BEGROTING 1992
MEERJARENBEGROTING 1993-1996
Concern

Concern BEGROTING 1992

GEMEENTE
DORDRECHT

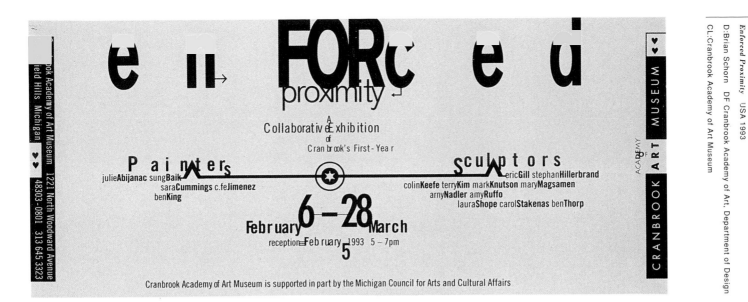

Invitation Card インビテーション・カード

Enforced Proximity USA 1993

D:Brian Schorn DF:Cranbrook Academy of Art, Department of Design

CL:Cranbrook Academy of Art Museum

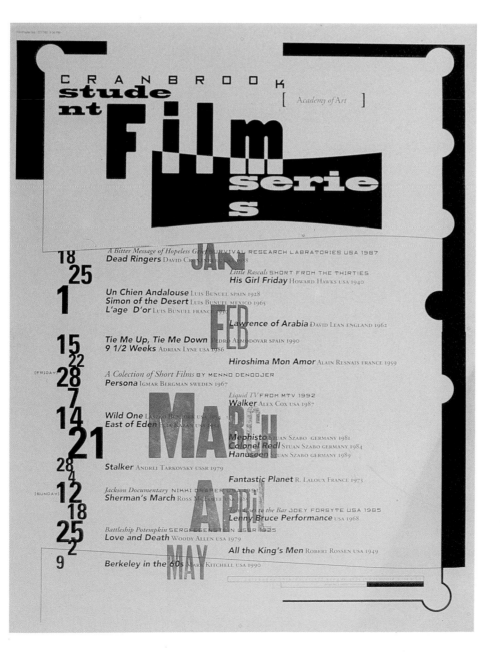

Poster ポスター

Student Film Series USA 1992

D:David Shields DF:Cranbrook Academy of Art, Department of Design

CL:Cranbrook Academy of Art Studio Council

Poster ポスター

AICP MOMA USA 1990
AD,CW:Richard Poulin D,CW:Rosemary Simpkins
DF:Richard Poulin Design Group CL:AICP MOMA

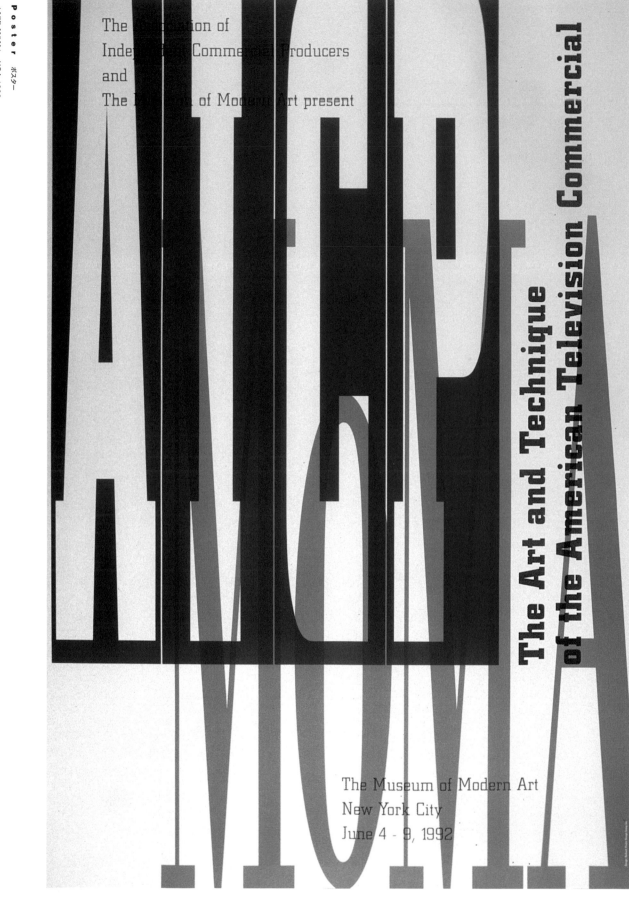

The Association of
Independent Commercial Producers
and
The Museum of Modern Art present

The Art and Technique
of the American Television Commercial

The Museum of Modern Art
New York City
June 4 - 9, 1992

Poster ポスター
Count Down UK 1992
AD.D:Terry Jones TY:Alan Kitchins
DF:Instant Design CL:Terry Jones and Associates

2/50

Record Packaging レコードパッケージ

Newspeak "Unperson" UK 1993

AD.D:The Designers Republic DF:The Designers Republic

CL:Gift Records

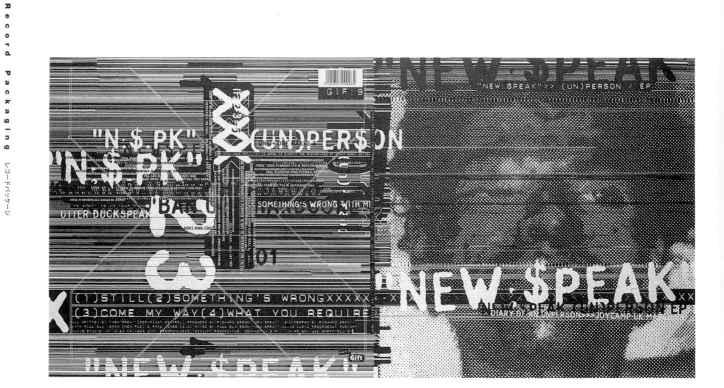

Record レコード

Pop Will Eat Itself "Bulletproof" UK 1992

AD.D:The Designers Republic DF:The Designers Republic

CL:RCA Records

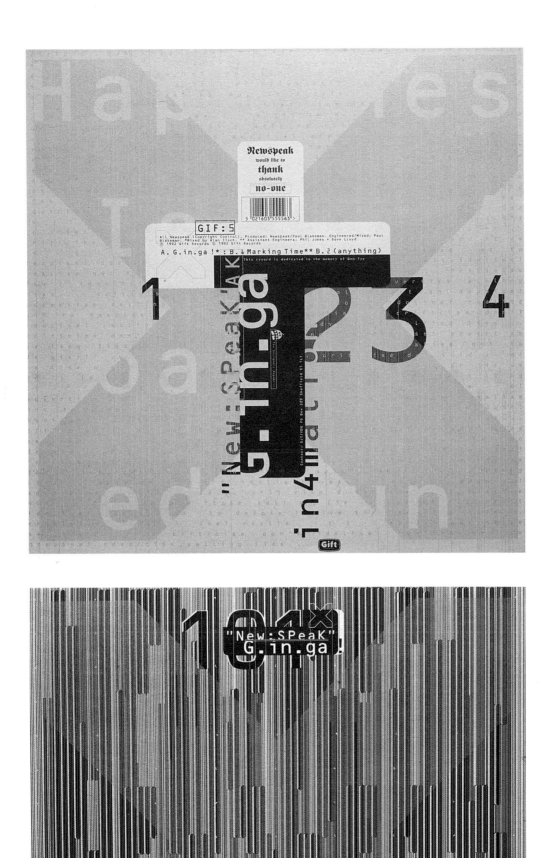

Record Packaging レコードパッケージ

Newspeak "GI. NG. A" UK 1992

AD,D:The Designers Republic　DF:The Designers Republic

CL:Gift Records

Poster ポスター

Takenobu Igarashi USA 1991

AD.D.CW:Richard Poulin P:Takenobu Igarashi

DF:Richard Poulin Design Group CL:American Institute of Graphic Arts, New York

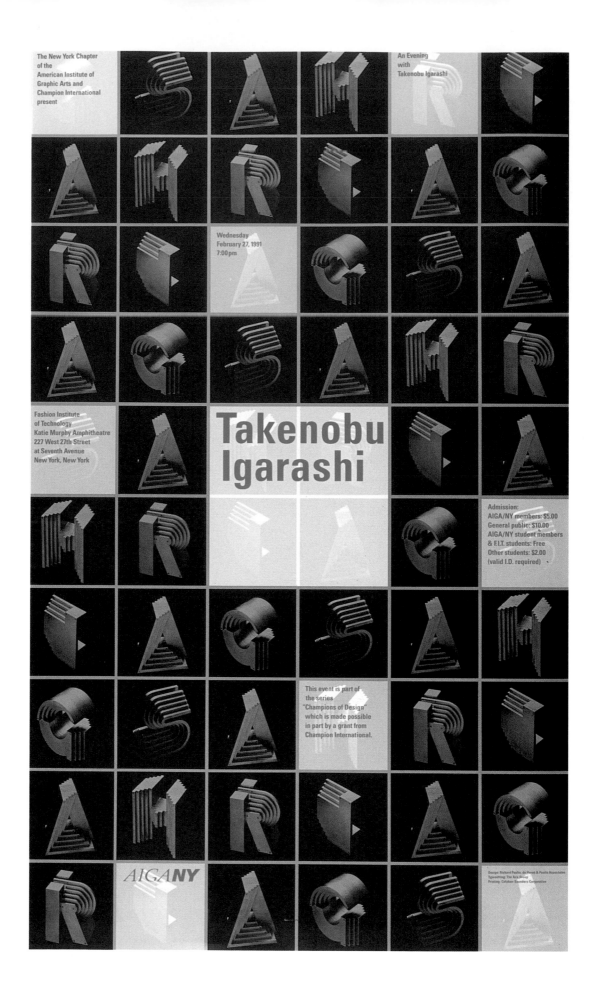

Poster ポスター

"Centre d'Architecture", Bordeaux, "Arc en Rêve" 1992　France 1992
AD,D:Philippe Apeloig
CL:Arc en Rêve, Bordeaux 1992

Catalogue カタログ

A is not an a /A is Geen £/ The Netherlands 1990

AD,D:Henrik Barends

CL:Van Reekummuseum, Apeldoorn DF:Studio Henrik Barends

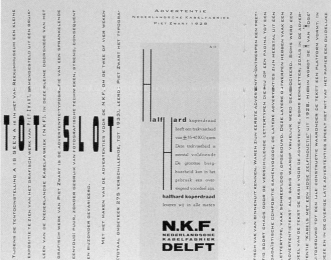

Book Cover ブックカバー

Maximaal The Netherlands 1989

AD,D:Henrik Barends TY:Astrid Klaasse-Bos

DF:Studio Henrik Barends CL:in de Knipscheer Publishers

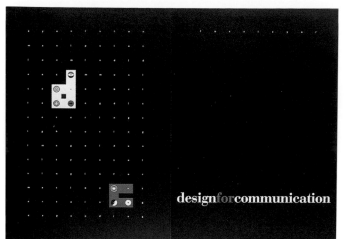

designforcommunication

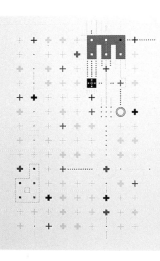

humanities

designformanufacture

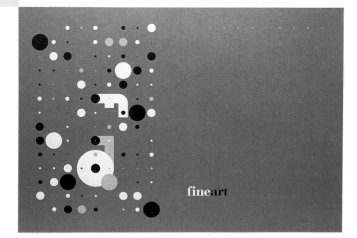

fineart

Brochure Spreads ブローシュアページ

Royal College of Art Report UK 1992

CD,D:Peter Grundy DF:Grundy & Northedge

CL:Royal College of Art London

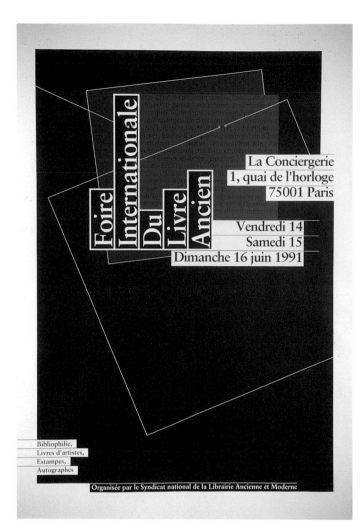

Poster ポスター

Foire Internationale du Livre Ancien a la Conciergerie, Paris France 1992

AD,D:Philippe Apeloig

CL:Syndicat National de la Librairie Ancienne et Moderne 1991

Poster ポスター

Executive Perspectives USA 1990

AD,D:Richard Poulin D:Mieko Oda

DF:Richard Poulin Design Group CL:IBM

9e

amsterdams

vliegerfeest

organisatie en info:vliegerwinkel Vliegertuig Gasthuismolensteeg 8 Amsterdam

za 30 | zo 31 mei 92

Recreatiegebied Spaarnwoude/Houtrak
Haarlem - Halfweg - Amsterdam
Bereikbaar met bus 80
Parkeer/kampeerplaatsen aanwezig

met   bekende Nederlandse vliegeraars
en hun vliegermodellen, een
speciaal stuntvliegerterrein,
muziek, kindertheater,
acrobaten, een vliegerwerkplaats
en vele andere activiteiten

en   op zaterdagavond
het nachtvliegeren en
live-muziek vanaf
circa 21.00 uur

Poster ポスター
Amsterdam Kite Festival The Netherlands 1992
AD,D:Frans Lieshout   DF:Design Connection, Amsterdam
CL:Vliegertuig

Press Release Folder プレスリリース・フォルダー
An Exhibition of the Work of Philippe Apeloig France 1991
AD,D:Philippe Apeloig
CL:Philippe Apeloig Design

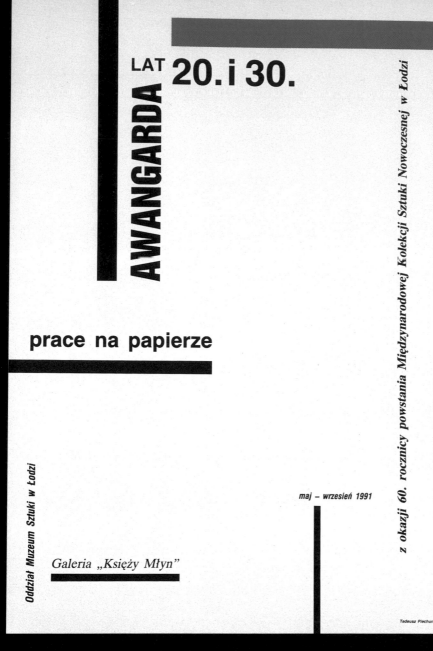

LAT **20. i 30.**

AWANGARDA

z okazji 60. rocznicy powstania Międzynarodowej Kolekcji Sztuki Nowoczesnej w Łodzi

prace na papierze

maj – wrzesień 1991

Oddział Muzeum Sztuki w Łodzi

Galeria „Księży Młyn"

Tadeusz Piechura

Zofia Lipecka

Muzeum Sztuki w Łodzi · Galeria „Księży Młyn" ul. Przędzalniana 72

Natura odzwierciedlona · Nature reflected

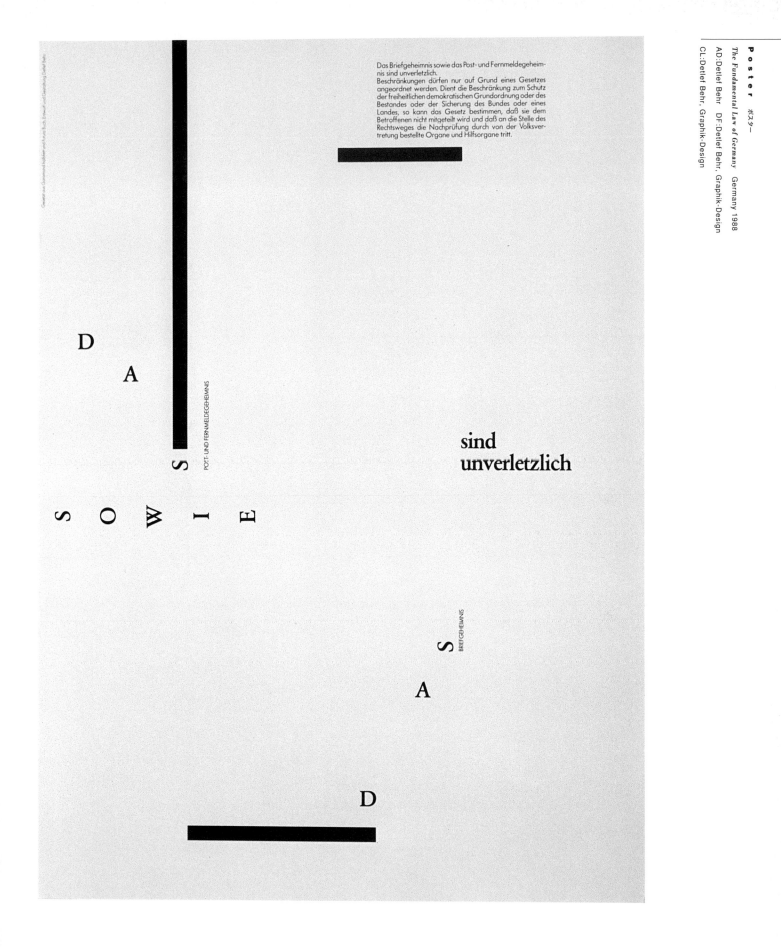

Poster ポスター

The Fundamental Law of Germany   Germany 1988
AD:Detlef Behr   DF:Detlef Behr, Graphik-Design
CL:Detlef Behr, Graphik-Design

Poster ポスター
You are Next USA 199
D:Joan Dobkin DF:Cranbrook Academy of Art, Department of Design
CL:Student Project

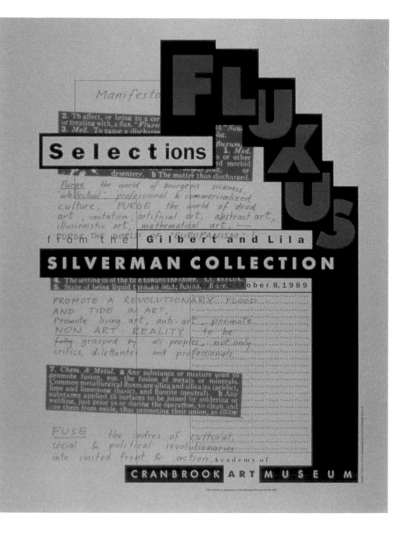

Poster ポスター
Fluxus Exhibition USA 1989
AD,D:Katherine McCoy DF:McCoy & McCoy Associates
CL:Cranbrook Academy of Art Museum

Poster ポスター

Visualize The Future Switzerland 1992
AD,D,I:Cornel Windlin
DF:Cornel Windlin CL:Parco

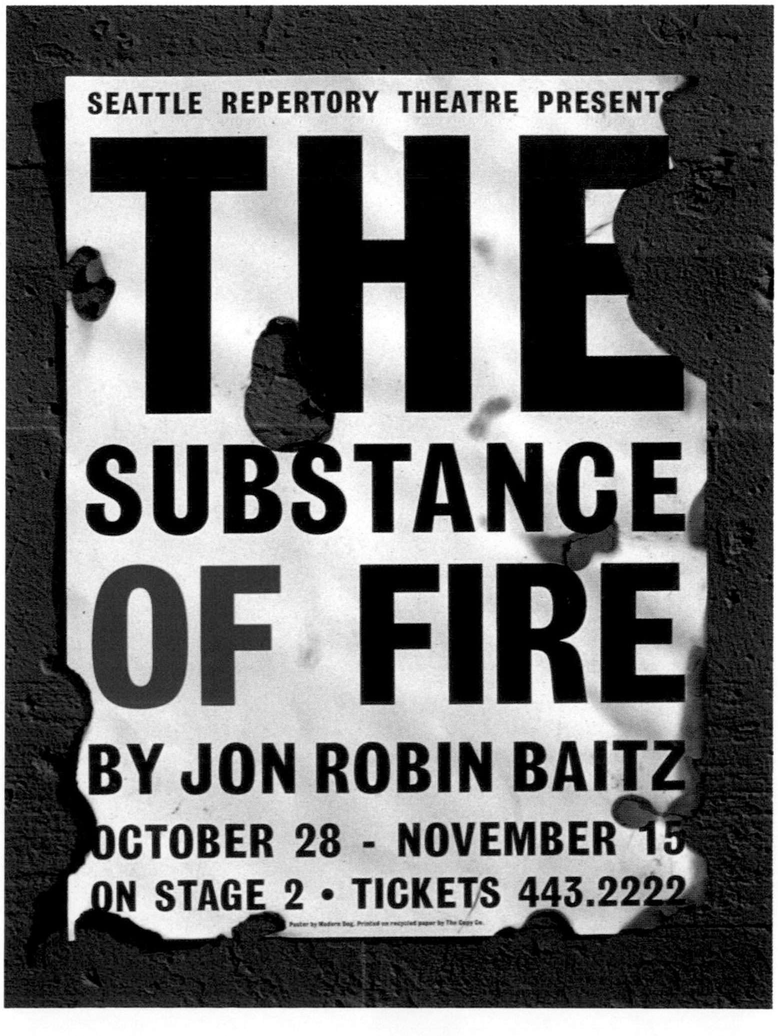

Poster ポスター

The Substance of Fire USA 1992
CD:Douglas Hughes AD, D:Robynne Raye
DF:Modern Dog CL:Seattle Repertory Theatre

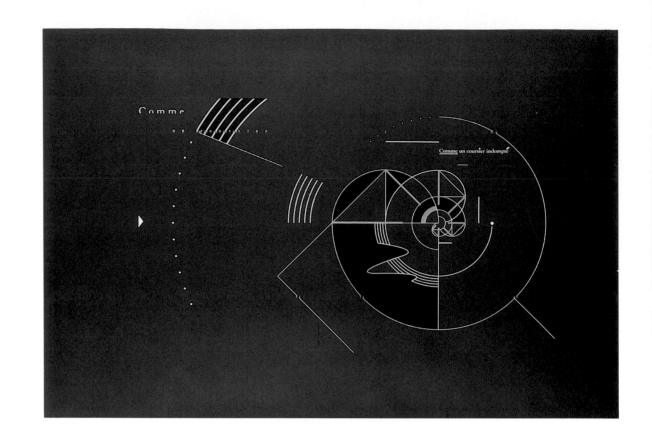

Book Cover ブックカバー

Comme un Coursier Indomate   France 1987

AD.D:Philippe Apeloig

CL:Imprimerie Nationale

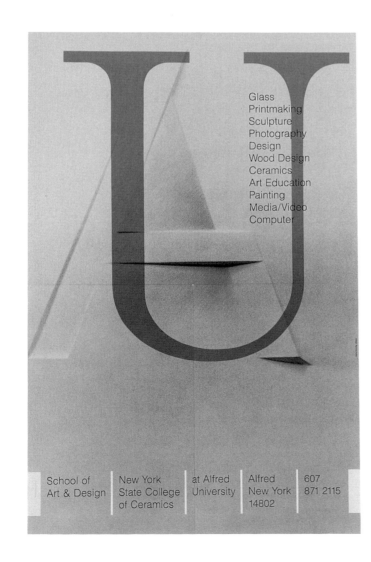

Poster ポスター

Alfred University   USA 1987

AD.D.P:Ramona Hutko   DF:Ramona Hutko Design

CL:Alfred University

P o s t e r s ポスター

Shirazeh Houshiary, Sue Coe Police State　UK 1988-1989
AD,D:Mervyn Kurlansky　D:Robert Dunnet　P:Nick Turner
DF:Pentagram Design　CL:Museum of Modern Art, Oxford

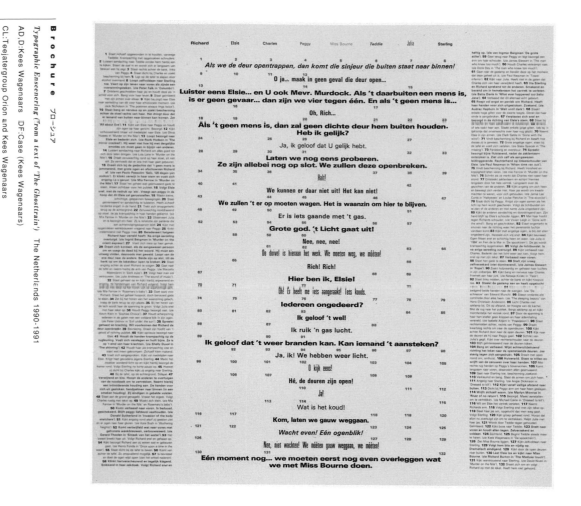

Sti ll Such

James Salter

Book *
"Still Such" USA 1992
D:Stephen Doyle P:Duane Michals
DF:Drenttel Doyle Partners CL:William Drenttel New York

Still Such

Down Fifth with the tail-lights, dark,
the wet street gleaming, city where
I always lived, school and the rest:
curly-haired friend confiding what he'd
done with Faith in her parents'

Inge und Heinz
Krippner

VON LU*MZ*ZERN
U
NACH ERLANGEN

Staffelweg 4
D-8520 Erlangen
Tel.: 0 91 31/20 56 79

Greeting Card グリーティング・カード
Umzug Austria 1987
AD,D,CW:Sigi Ramoser DF:Ramoser Sigi
CL:Mr+Mrs. Krippner

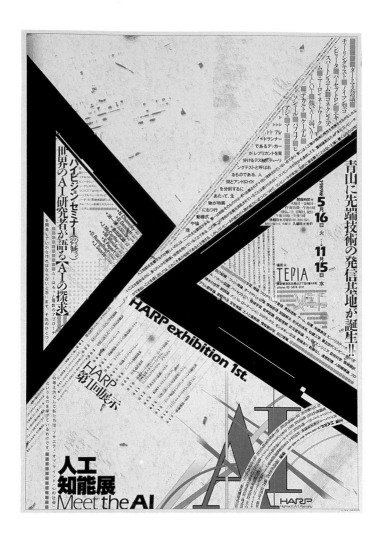

Poster ポスター

Meet The AI Japan 1989

D:Hitoshi Suzuki Typesetter:Kiyoaki Inoue

CL:HARP (Highteck Art Flanning)

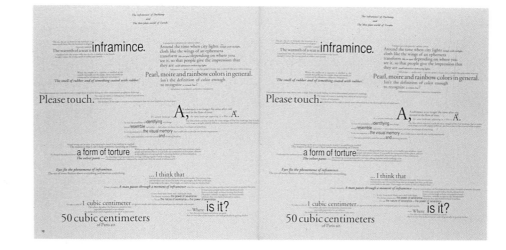

Artwork for 3D-Vision 立体視のためのアート作品

NEn No.2 · The things that eyes can see − a workshop about the 'thin world' of three-dimensional vision:

The 'Inframince' of Duchamp and The 'thin plate world' of Taruho Japan 1992

Artist:Yukio Fujimoto + Yasuhiko Nagahara CL:ARTLAB, Canon

Depuis 1973, Tréfle intervient sur le marché de. l'image et de l'identité d'entreprise. *(corporate identity)*

Tréfle propose aux directions générales, aux directions de la communication,

aux secrétariats généraux, aux directeurs des ressources humaines, aux directeurs financiers

le principe d'une spécialisation à l'intérieur de laquelle tous les domaines sont

maîtrisés pour offrir un service complet et modulable.

Cette démarche, contrastant avec celle des intervenants généralistes,

est résolument tournée vers le haut de gamme.

Toutes nos énergies convergent dans le même sens : **créer,** (concevoir, innover, imaginer) · · · · au service de l'image · · · · · · · · **publique** · · · · · · des entreprises.

Avec des approches sur mesure et en profondeur, nos équipes privilégient **l'écoute active.**

Responsables de leur mission de bout en bout, elles sont capables d'intégrer dans la création toutes les contraintes

économiques, culturelles, sociales, psychologiques de chaque entreprise.

Poster ポスター

Call for Entries　UK 1991

D:David Quay　DF:David Quay Design

CL:Society of Typographic Designers

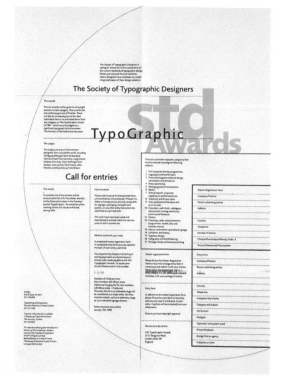

Poster ポスター

ADA in Focus　USA 1992

D:Robert Beerman　D.P:Robert Brown

DF:Sasaki Associates/Graphic Design　CL:The Society for Environmental Graphic Design

The Society for Environmental Graphic Design

S E G D is offering three one-day seminars across the country to help designers and allied professionals interpret, react, and respond to the **A D A**. The legislation has a dizzying array of implications for many design fields–implications that are as far-reaching as they are confusing.

IF YOU'VE EVER DESIGNED A SIGN–OR PLAN TO DESIGN ANOTHER–YOU NEED TO KNOW THE EFFECTS OF THE **A D A** ON YOUR CLIENTS, YOUR PROJECTS, AND YOUR ENTIRE BUSINESS PRACTICE BECAUSE ON JANUARY 26, 1992 THE DESIGN AND SPECIFYING OF SIGNAGE CHANGED FOREVER.

GAUGING THE IMPACT OF
THE AMERICANS WITH DISABILITIES ACT

APRIL 4 – WASHINGTON, DC
APRIL 11 – CHICAGO
APRIL 25 – SAN FRANCISCO

S E G D　A D A　EDUCATION SEMINARS

SPONSORED BY THE SOCIETY FOR ENVIRONMENTAL GRAPHIC DESIGN (S E G D)
IN CONJUNCTION WITH THE FOLLOWING GROUPS

ATBCB
AIA
IDSA
ASLA
ASID
AIGA
ACD
IBD
BOMA

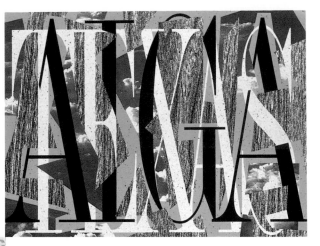

Postcard ポストカード
AIGA Postcard   USA 1992
AD,D:Brad Grulke   D,I:David Kampa
DF:Heatly Associates   CL:AIGA Texas

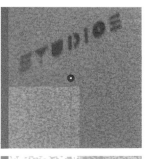

If you care about graphic design you belong in the AIGA. The American Institute of Graphic Arts advances the graphic design profession through competitions, exhibitions, publications, professional seminars, educational activities, and projects in the public interest. Please complete the post card provided and let us know what the AIGA can do for you or what you can do for the AIGA (all AIGA chapters are run by members for members, therefore you can participate on a level that is meaningful).

Exchange ideas and information about graphic design.

Join AIGA Texas.

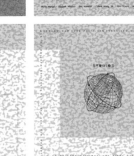

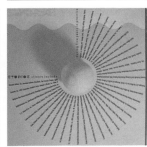

Brochure Folder   ブローシュア・フォルダー
Studios Announcement   USA 1991
AD,D,P:Jeff Fabian, Jean Kane, Sam Shelton   CW:Bruce Danzer
DF:Kinetik Communication Graphics   CL:Studios Architecture

Poster ポスター

666 Japan 1991

AD.D:Tomohiko Nagakura

DF:Sun-Ad CL:Takeo

BESTIA DE MARI ASCENDENS SEPTEM CAPITUM ET DECEM CORNUUM
DECEMQUE DIADEMATUM, CUJUS PLAGA CURATUR, DEUM BLASPHEMAT
ET SANCTOS DEBELLAT. ALTERAQUE BESTIA DUORUM CORNUUM DE
TERRA ASCENDENS ILLI MAXIME FAVET, COGENS FIERI ET ADORARI EJUS
IMAGINEM, HABERIQUE CHARACTEREM NOMINIS EJUS. 1. ET VIDI DE MARI
BESTIAM ASCENDENTEM HABENTEM CAPITA SEPTEM, ET CORNUA DECEM,
ET SUPER CORNUA EJUS DECEM DIADEMATA, ET SUPER CAPITA EJUS
NOMINA BLASPHEMIÆ. 2. ET BESTIA QUAM VIDI, SIMILIS ERAT PARDO, ET
PEDES EJUS SICUT PEDES URSI, ET OS EJUS SICUT OS LEONIS. ET DEDIT
ILLI DRACO VIRTUTEM SUAM ET POTESTATEM MAGNAM. 3. ET VIDI UNUM
DE CAPITIBUS SUIS QUASI OCCISUM IN MORTEM; ET PLAGA MORTIS EJUS
CURATA EST. ET ADMIRATA EST UNIVERSA TERRA POST BESTIAM. 4. ET
ADORAVERUNT DRACONEM, QUI DEDIT POTESTATEM BESTIÆ; ET ADORA-
VERUNT BESTIAM DICENTES : QUIS SIMILIS BESTIÆ? ET QUIS POTERIT
PUGNARE CUM EA? 5. ET DATUM EST EI OS LOQUENS MAGNA, ET BLAS-
PHEMIAS ; ET DATA EST EI POTESTAS FACERE MENSES QUADRAGINTA
DUOS. 6. ET APERUIT OS SUUM IN BLASPHEMIAS AD DEUM, BLASPHEMARE
NOMEN EJUS, ET TABERNACULUM EJUS, ET EOS, QUI IN CŒLO HABITANT.
7. ET EST DATUM ILLI BELLUM FACERE CUM SANCTIS, ET VINCERE EOS. ET
DATA EST ILLI POTESTAS IN OMNEM TRIBUM, ET POPULUM, ET LINGUAM,
ET GENTEM. 8. ET ADORAVERUNT EAM OMNES QUI INHABITANT TERRAM,
QUORUM NON SUNT SCRIPTA NOMINA IN LIBRO VITÆ AGNI, QUI OCCISUS
EST AB ORIGINE MUNDI. 9. SI QUIS HABET AUREM, AUDIAT. 10. QUI IN CAP-
TIVITATEM DUXERIT, IN CAPTIVITATEM VADET ; QUI IN GLADIO OCCIDERIT,
OPORTET EUM GLADIO OCCIDI. HIC EST PATIENTIA, ET FIDES SANCTORUM.
11. ET VIDI ALIAM BESTIAM ASCENDENTEM DE TERRA, ET HABEBAT COR-
NUA DUO SIMILIA AGNI, ET LOQUEBATUR SICUT DRACO. 12. ET POTESTATEM
PRIORIS BESTIÆ OMNEM FACIEBAT IN CONSPECTU EJUS : ET FECIT TE-
RRAM, ET HABITANTES IN EA, ADORARE BESTIAM PRIMAM, CUJUS CURATA
EST PLAGA MORTIS. 13. ET FECIT SIGNA MAGNA, UT ETIAM IGNEM FACE-
RET DE CŒLO DESCENDERE IN TERRAM IN CONSPECTU HOMINUM. 14. ET
SEDUXIT HABITANTES IN TERRA PROPTER SIGNA QUÆ DATA SUNT ILLI
FACERE IN CONSPECTU BESTIÆ, DICENS HABITANTIBUS IN TERRA, UT
FACIANT IMAGINEM BESTIÆ QUÆ HABET PLAGAM GLADII, ET VIXIT. 15. ET
DATUM EST ILLI UT DARET SPIRITUM IMAGINI BESIÆ, ET UT LOQUATUR
IMAGO BESTIÆ : ET FACIAT UT QUICUMQUE NON ADORAVERINT IMAGINEM
BESTIÆ, OCCIDANTUR. 16. ET FACIET OMNES PUSILLOS, ET MAGNOS, ET
DIVITES, ET PAUPERES, ET LIBEROS, ET SERVOS HABERE CHARACTEREM
IN DEXTERA MANU SUA, AUT IN FRONTIBUS SUIS. 17. ET NE QUIS POSSIT
EMERE, AUT VENDERE, NISI QUI HABET CHARACTEREM, AUT NOMEN BES-
TIÆ, AUT NUMERUM NOMINIS EJUS. 18. HIC SAPIENTIA EST. QUI HABET
INTELLECTUM, COMPUTET NUMERUM BESTIÆ. NUMERUS ENIM HOMINIS
EST : ET NUMERUS EJUS SEXCENTI SEXAGINTA SEX.

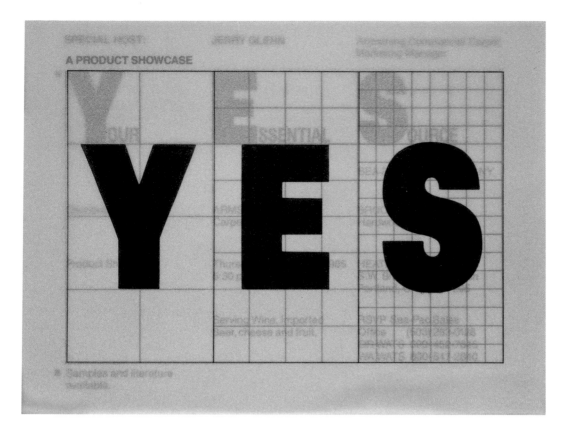

Stationery ステーショナリー

Yes USA 1985
AD:Rick Eiber D:RED Staff
DF:Rick Eiber Design (RED) CL:Sea Pac Sales

Promotional Packaging プロモーションパッケージ

One Voice - Art in Music Japan 1992
AD,D:Keisuke Unosawa DF:Keisuke Unosawa
CL:Videoarts Japan

Poster ポスター

An Exhibition of the Design of Philippe Apeloig at the Centre d'Architecture, Bordeaux, 1991.

France 1991

AD,D:Philippe Apeloig

Diary Cover ダイアリーカバー

l'Association Francaise d'Action Artistique　France 1992

AD,D:Philippe Apeloig

CL:l'Association Francaise d'Action Artistique

Poster ポスター
Open Huis The Netherlands 1992
AD,D:Edvard Milnar P:Gerard Keuter
DF:Milnar Design CL:College voor Beroepsonderwijs Zwolle

Press Release Folder プレスリリース・フォルダー
Dance Company "Regine Chopinot" France 1988
AD,D:Philippe Apeloig
CL:Regine Chopinot

Catalogue カタログ

Haute Cuisine From The Lowlands The Netherlands 1987

AD,D:Frans Lieshout

CL:Robert van Rixtel

Poster ポスター

2.25 *Gert Dumbar*   USA 1992

AD,D,CW:Douglas Morris, Richard Poulin   DF:Richard Poulin Design Group

CL:American Institute of Graphic Arts, New York/Society of Environmental Graphic Design

The New York Chapter of the
American Institute of Graphic Arts
and the New York region of the
Society for Environmental Graphic Design
present an evening with

**Gert Dumbar of
Studio Dumbar, Netherlands.**

Fashion Institute
of Technology
Katie Murphy Amphitheatre
227 West 27th Street
at Seventh Avenue
New York City

Admission
$5 AIGA/SEGD members
$10 general public
AIGA/SEGD student members
and FIT students: free
$2 other students
with valid student I.D.

**Tuesday
25 February 1992
7:00 pm**

Poster ポスター

Millares, Saura, Tàpies   Poland 1990

AD,D,CW:Tadeusz Piechura   DF:Atelier Tadeusz Piechura

CL:Museum of Art, Lodzi

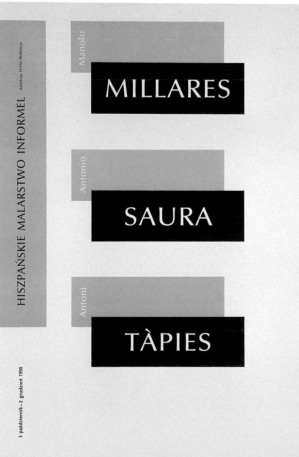

HISZPAŃSKIE MALARSTWO INFORMEL   Kolekcja IVAM-Walencja

Manolo
MILLARES

Antonio
SAURA

Antoni
TÀPIES

3 października – 2 grudzień 1990

Muzeum Sztuki, Łódź
ul. Więckowskiego 36

Poster ポスター
Advertising for Float Japan 1992
AD:Akio Okumura D:Emi Kajihara
DF:Packaging Create ©L:Inoue Yoshiten

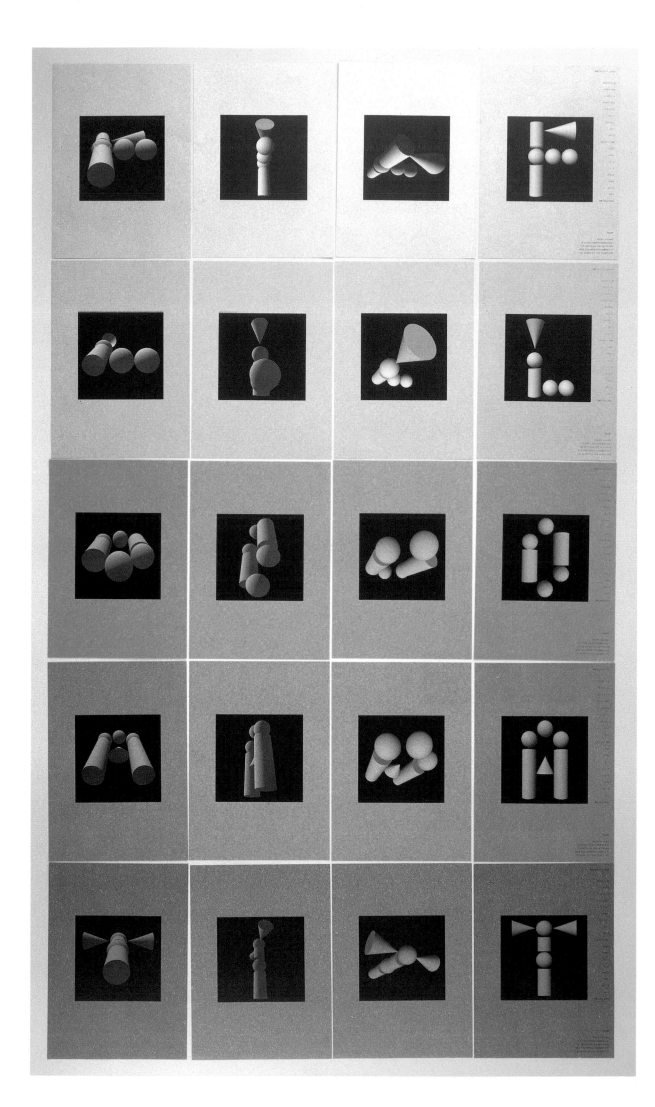

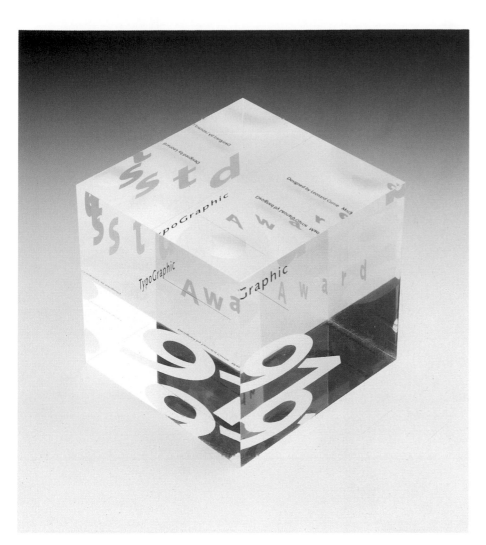

Trophy トロフィー
STD Award UK 1992
D:Leonard Currie F:George Taylor
DF:Leonard Currie Design CL:Society of Typographic Designers

Greeting Card グリーティング・カード
ICI Studio Events, 1993 USA 1992
AD,D:Michael McGinn AD:Takaaki Matsumoto
CL:Independent Curators

Poster ポスター

JCH Moving Announcement　USA 1989
AD,D,I:Takaaki Matsumoto
AD:Michael McGinn
CL:JCH Group

Poster ポスター

Rimbaud:Colour of Vowels　UK 1992
AD,D:Alan Kitching
CL:The Typography Workshop

Poster ポスター

Typuzzle UK 1992
AD.,D.:Peter Grundy, James Beveridge, Alan Kitching
DF.:Peter Grundy, James Beveridge, Alan Kitching   CL:Personal Project

Typuzzle : designed set and printed letterpress by James Beveridge/Peter Grundy/Alan Kitching at The Typography Workshop Clerkenwell London August 1992

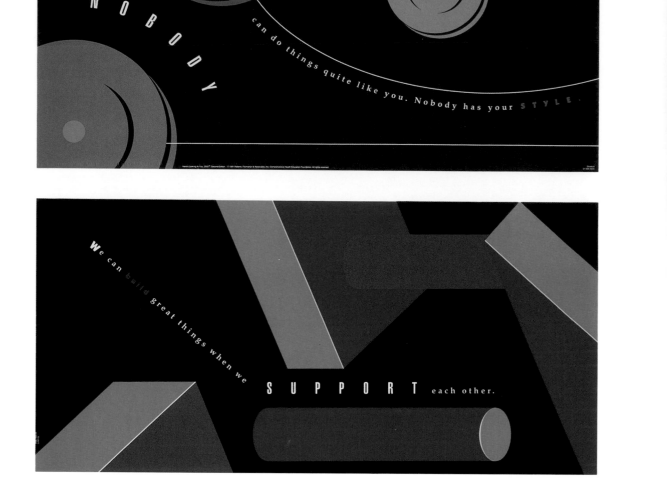

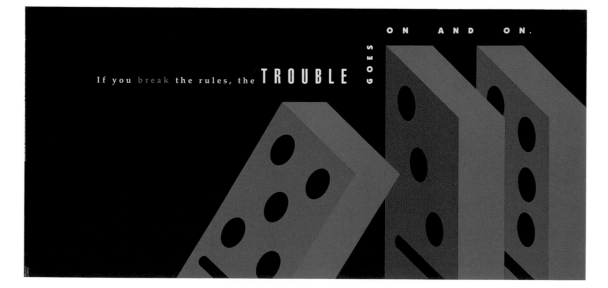

Posters ポスター

Drug Curriculum Message Poster Series   USA 1991

AD,D:John Hornall   AD,C,I:Julia LaPine   D,I:David Bates, Heidi Hatestad, Brian O'Neill   CW:Pamela Mason-Davey, Neil Starkman

DF:Hornall Anderson Des gn Works   CL:Roberts, Fitzmahan & Assocates/Comprehensive Health Education Foundation

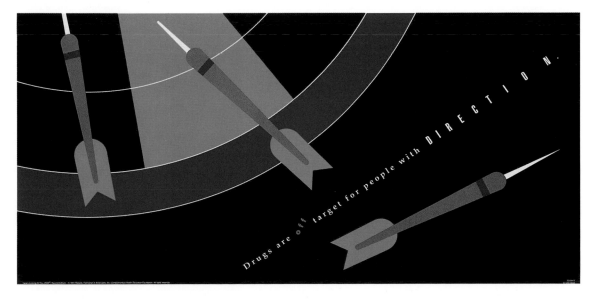

Poster ポスター

Handa Advertisement USA 1992

AD.D:Takaaki Matsumoto AD:Michael McGinn

CL:Perfect Marketing

Poster ポスター

SFADC Student Portfolio Review USA 1988

D.I:Mark Fox DF:BlackDog

CL:The San Francisco Art Directors Club

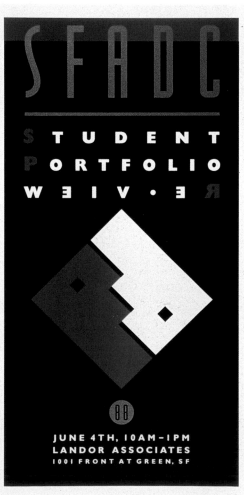

L is for Little.

The opposite of little is big.

Can you find the little circle?

little

big

Brochure Spread ブローシュアスペーシ

Andy Arrow's Alphabet Book USA 1991

AD,D:Rick Valicenti, Ilse Krause DF:Thirst

CL:Kathleen Krause

Poster ポスター

Saturday High　USA 1991

D:Rebeca Mendez　DF:Art Center College of Design, Design Office

CL:Art Center College of Design

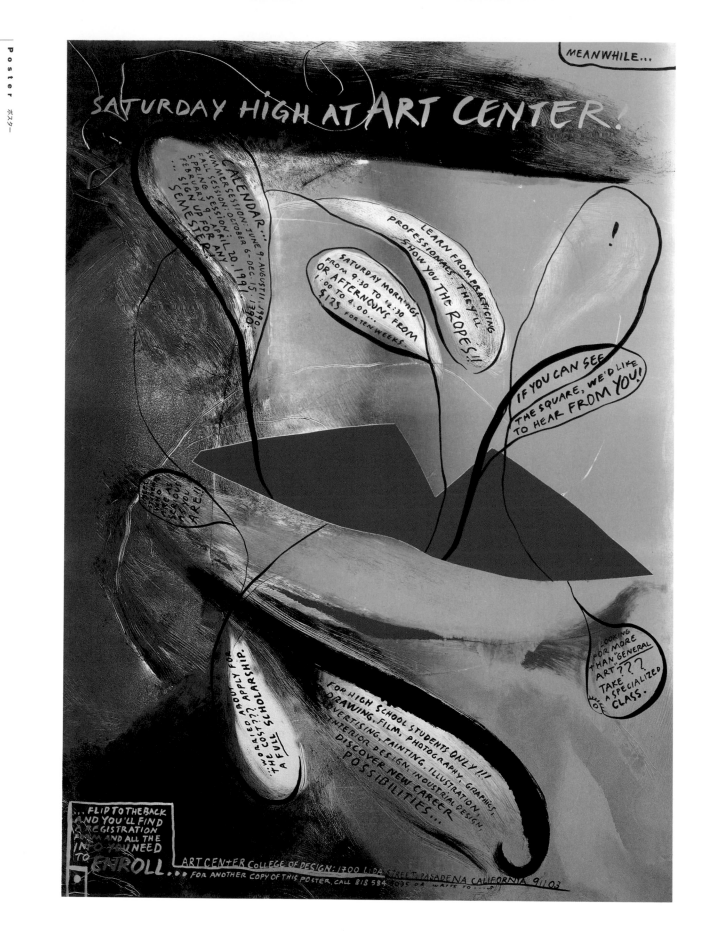

Poster ポスター

Contrary USA 1993

D:Fred Bower DF:Cranbrook Academy of Art, Department of Design

CL:Student Project

Catalogue カタログ

Type Promotion UK 1990

D:Leonard Currie DF:Leonard Currie

CL:Letraset

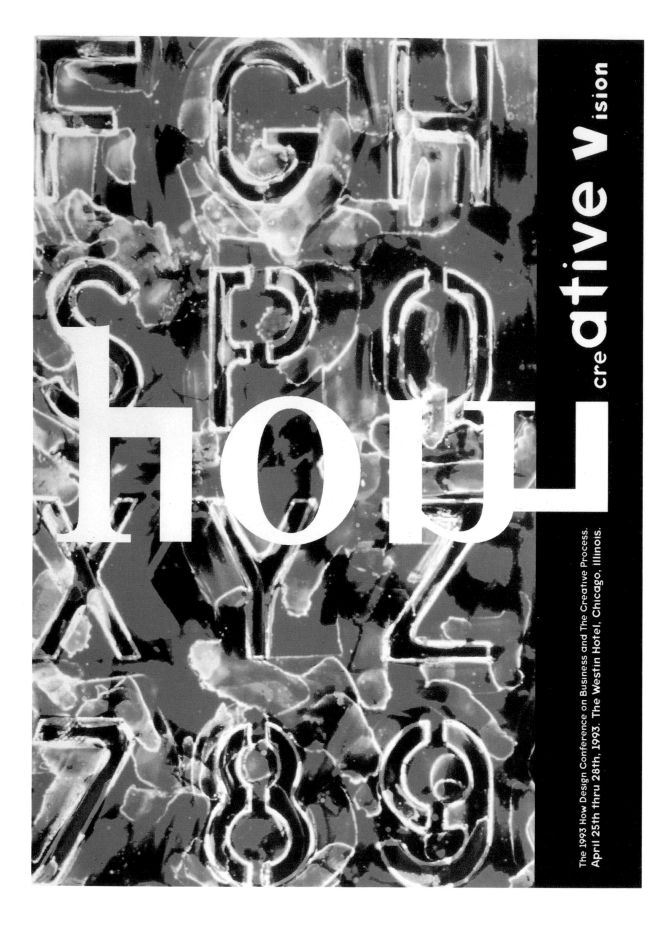

Postcard ポストカード
How Design Conference USA 1992
AD.D:Carlos Segura P:Photonica
CW:Bruce Charles & How DF:Segura CL:How Magazine

Pamphlet パンフレット

CAT Bldg Japan 1992

AD:Naomi Enami D:Masaki Kimura

P:Yoshihiko Minagawa CL:Too

Paper Bag 紙袋

Company Earth Japan 1992

AD,D:Keikc Ogasawa`a

CL:Earth

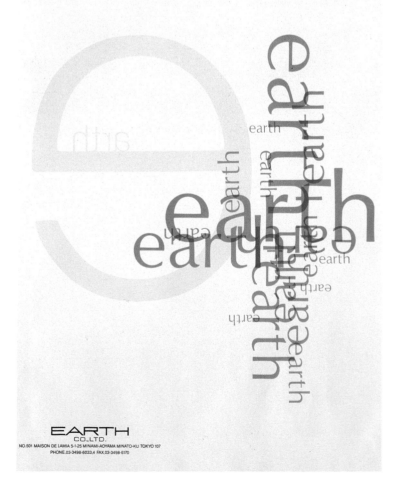

Direct Mail ダイレクトメール
'92 Spring Summer Collection Japan 1992
AD:Hisao Sugiura D:Yasunobu Kawajiri
DF:Studio Super Compass CL:Y's

Direct Mail ダイレクトメール
'92 Spring & Summer Exhibition Vol.1 Japan 1992
AD:Hisao Sugiura D:Yasunobu Kawajiri
DF:Studio Super Compass CL:Y's

Direct Mail ダイレクトメール
'92-'93 Autumn & Winter Exhibition Vol.1 Japan 1992
AD,D:Hisao Sugiura D:Toshio Matsuura
DF:Studio Super Compass CL:Y's

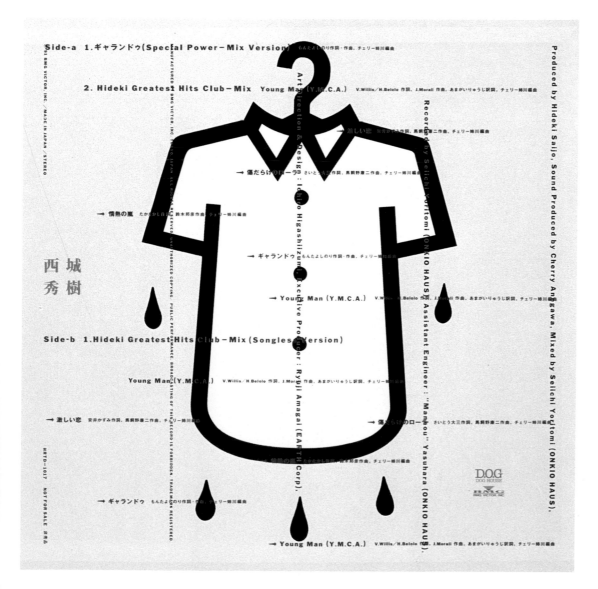

Record Packaging レコードパッケージ

Hideki House Japan 1991
AD,D:Ichiro Higashiizumi D:Shuichi Miyagishi, Megumi Takeuchi
DF:Huia Media Design CL:BMG Victor

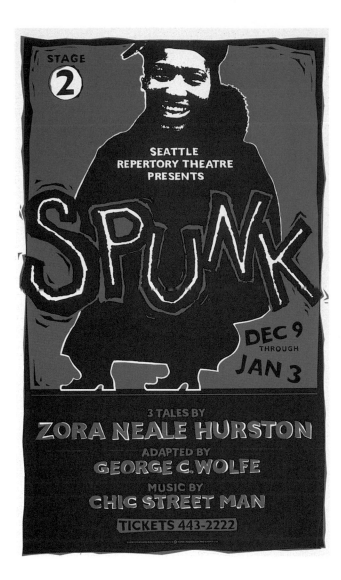

Poster ポスター

Spunk USA 1992

CD:Rich Gerdes   AD:Robynne Raye   AD.D.I:Vittorio Costarella

DF:Modern Dog   CL:Seattle Repertory Theatre

Poster ポスター

John Sayles Baits The Hook USA 1992

AD.D.I.CW:John Sayles

DF:Sayles Graphic Design   CL:Sayles Graphic Design

tag

Poster ポスター
Carnival Australia 1991
AD,D,I:Andrew Hoyne
DF:Andrew Hoyne Cesign   CL:Black Match Hotel

Magazine Advertisement 雑誌広告

Power Channel Japan 1991

AD,D:Ichiro Higashiizumi

DF:Huia Media Design CL:Autobahn/Parco

CD Packaging ＣＤパッケージ
Love Is Blue Japan 1993
CD:Comoesta Yaegashi AD,D:Ichiro Higashiizumi
P:Shinichi Itoh DF:Huia Media Design CL:Teichiku Records

Poster ポスター
Every Good Boy Live At USA 1992
AD,D:Rudy Vanderlans DF:Emigre
CL:Emigre

Pamphlets パンフレット

Venous News Vol.3/4 ―Japan 1992／1993

CD:Hiroshi Hasegawa, Kenji Hanaue　AD,D:Yoshiro Kajitani

D:Michiko Arakawa　P:Jun Konta　DF:Kajitani Design Room　CL:Urayasu City

Poster ポスター

Urayasu City 10th Anniversary Festival　Japan 1991

CD:Hiroshi Hasegawa, Kenji Hanaue　AD,D:Yoshiro Kajitani

D:Michiko Arakawa　I:Suzy Amakane　DF:Kajitani Design Room　CL:Urayasu City

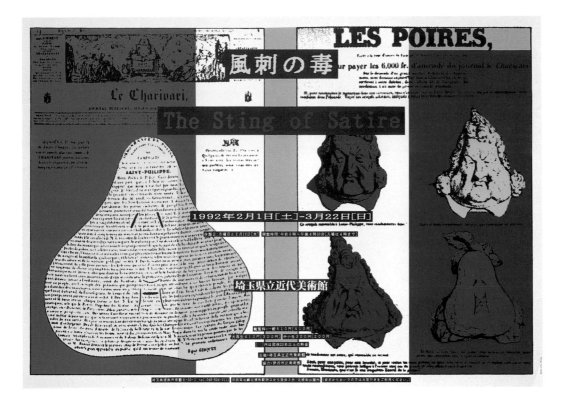

Poster ポスター

The Sting of Satire　Japan 1992
AD,D:Kijuro Yahagi
CL:The Museum of Modern Art, Saitama

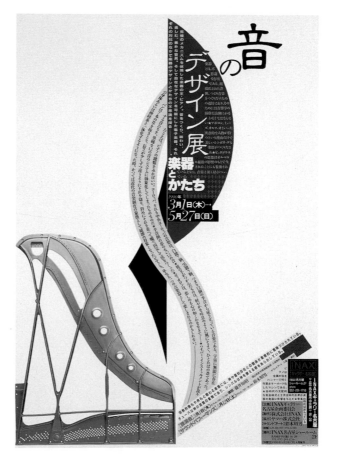

Poster ポスター

Mannequin Exhibition　Japan 1990
D:Hitoshi Suzuki　P:Hitoshi Fugo
CL:Inax HARP (Highteck Art Planning)

Poster ポスター

Sound Design Exhibition　Japan 1990
D:Hitoshi Suzuki　Typesetter:Kiyoaki Inoue
CL:Inax

camote
people

Ishquat
Batan Islands
● Batan I.
Sabtang I.
Balintang I.
Balintang Channel
Babuyan I.
Calayan I.
Calayan
Dalupiri I. Babuyan Islands
Fuga I. Camiguin I.
Babuyan Channel

LUZON

There may be no telephones, few stores and too many wild storms in the Batan Islands. But as long as the yams and the sweet potatoes continue to take root, so will the most isolated islanders in the Philippines

SOUTH   PACIFIC

CHINA   MANILA ■   OCEAN

SEA

BY **JON MILLER**

PHOTOGRAPHY BY **KEVIN HAMDORF**

We are in an open boat, scoop-bottomed, tippy, full of rice sacks and dried fish, old bicycles and people. It is mid-morning; the sea beyond the reef-line is black. Dark clouds rush from Sabtang, where we've been, to Ivana, where we're going. The surface of the sea is like a blanket thrown over a fitful sleeper. We pitch forward but are thrust to the side by an elbow; we fall as the elbow falls and catch a soft rolling hip coming up. Then a knee comes from nowhere and butts us back. A bent leg is extended and for a moment we rip along its length like a sailboat in a good wind. Then the sleeper half wakes and rises, groggy, and we ride up a great heaving chest that carries us higher and higher, then falls, exhausted, behind us.

Magazine Spread 雑誌ページ

Camote People Hong Kong 1992

AD:Percy Chung CW:Jen Miller

DF:Emphasis (Hong Kong) CL:Cathay Pacific Airways

ON LOCATION WITH LILIAN PAN,
THE INSCRUTABLE, INDOMITABLE GRAND LADY
OF MODERN CHINESE LITERATURE

Lilian likes red

BY LYNN PAN | PHOTOGRAPHY BY BASIL PAO

Magazine Spread 雑誌ページ

Lilian Likes Red Hong Kong 1992

AD,D:Andra Koura P:Basil Pao CW:Lynn Pan

DF:Emphasis (Hong Kong) CL:Cathay Pacific Airways

Postcard ポストカード
Raymond Hong Kong 1992
CL:Wong Ting Kit

Poster ポスター
Tears Japan 1992
AD:Keizo Matui
C:Yuko Araki CL:Dai Nippon Printing

Book 本

The Terminator Line UK 1991

AD,D,P,I:Jake Tilson

CL:Atlas

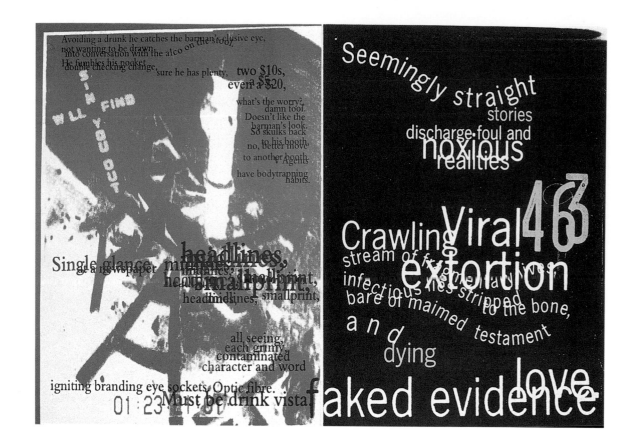

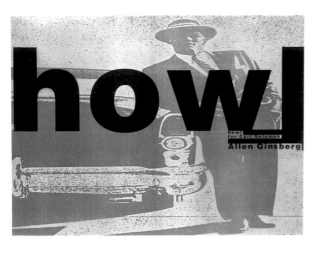

Book ＊

"The How!" From Allen Ginsberg Germany 1991
AD,D:Peter Biler   DF:Peter Biler
CL:Hochschuse Für Gestaltung Offenbach

Magazine Spread 雑誌ページ

"Output" USA 1991

D:Fred Bower, Bob Berds, Jim Ozolins, Klynn Dunkin

DF:Cranbrook Academy of Art, Department of Design   CL:Cranbrook Academy of Art

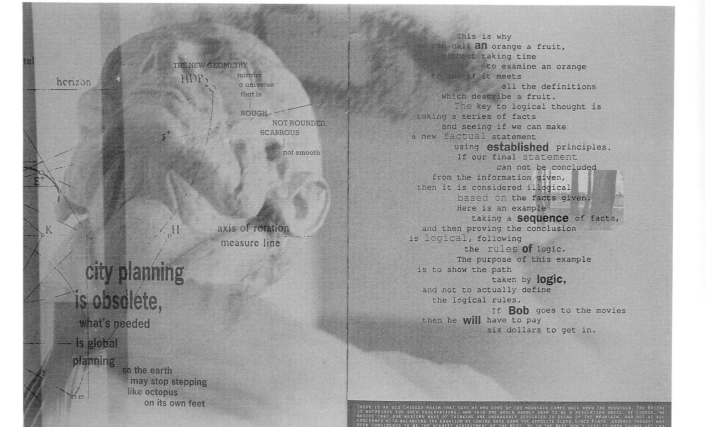

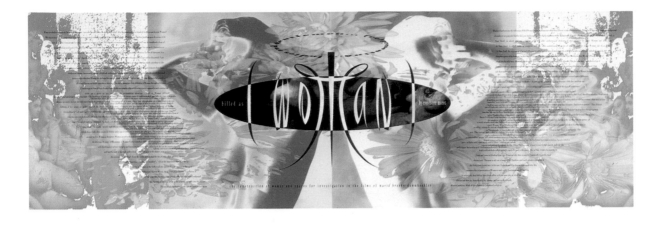

Magazine Spreads 雑誌ページ

"Beach Culture Magazine" May/June '91 USA 1991

AD.:David Carson P:Steve Sherman

DF:David Carson Design CL:Beach Culture Magazine

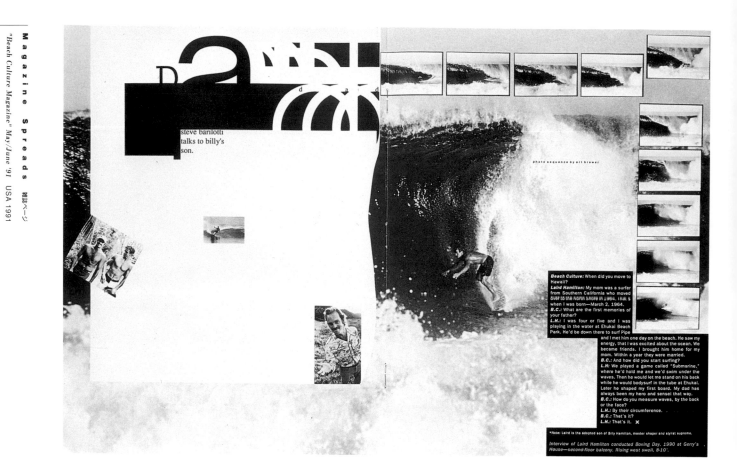

steve bartlotti talks to billy's son.

photo sequence by art brewer

Beach Culture: When did you move to Hawaii?

Laird Hamilton: My mom was a surfer from Southern California who moved over to the north shore in 1964. That is when I was born—March 2, 1964.

B.C.: What are the first memories of your father?

L.H.: I was four or five and I was playing in the water at Ehukai Beach Park. He'd be down there to surf Pipe and I met him one day on the beach. He saw my energy, that I was excited about the ocean. We became friends. I brought him home for my mom. Within a year they were married.

B.C.: And how did you start surfing?

L.H: We played a game called "Submarine," where he'd hold me and we'd swim under the waves. Then he would let me stand on his back while he would bodysurf in the tube at Ehukai. Later he shaped my first board. My dad has always been my hero and sensei that way.

B.C.: How do you measure waves, by the back or the face?

L.H.: By their circumference.

B.C.: That's it?

L.H.: That's it. ✖

Note: Laird is the adopted son of Billy Hamilton, master shaper and stylist supreme.

Interview of Laird Hamilton conducted Boxing Day, 1990 at Gerry's House—second-floor balcony. Rising west swell, 8-10'.

THE BEST BEACH BARS IN THE WORLD, PART ONE.

beach bars

You can always find a bar. But finding a beach bar, that's another story.

Beach bars are those classic places where real beach people hang. Where it's cool to have sand on your feet, to check out the ocean and to wear shorts year-round. And, best of all, where you can walk out the door and fall face-first into the sand.

Like these!

Crazy Charlie's and Chicho's, Virginia Beach, Virginia.

Virginia Beach is every East Coast college kid's party dream, with many bars that even the most avid party animal will remember long after graduation. Located on the infamous Va Beach "block" are two beach bars of unusual integrity: Crazy Charlie's and Chicho's. Charlie's gets the 25 to 35 crowd; Chicho's attracts the younger, more dedicated night-lifers.

But don't—repeat—don't go to these bars if you're shy, 'cause you just might be standing nipple-to-nipple with the person of your dreams. If you can't get laid in one of these two establishments, it's because you didn't try very hard.

Bring earplugs and a voracious appetite. Chicho's special spicy pizza and Charlie's cheeseburgers are both dripping with flavor. And let the locals buy you

a beer. They'd love to.

The favorite pastimes include chest pounding; ritually slugging down a bizarre concoction called a Bloody Brain; schmoozing with the young F-16 pilots from nearby Norfolk; and participating in the popular weekly contest called "Safe Sex Night." Contestants, both male and female, must accomplish some twisted feat for an adoring and loud crowd. The coveted grand prize is a sex survival bag consisting of a rubber ducky T-shirt, two condoms, wash rag and soap, and a postcard, presumably so you can write home.

Danny's, St. Simon Island, Georgia.

This quaint little seaside resort village's newest beach bar opened only last year. Already it's the favorite local hangout, not to mention showcase for up-and-coming progressive Georgia acts such as the All Good Music Company, the Aqua Velvet Cheese Band, Tommy Thompson, the Flying Buffalos, Nathan Sheperd and the Grapes, and the Cosmic Funk Pups. Because of these bands, Danny's is as popular with tourists from Athens and Atlanta as with St. Simon residents.

"There's no sign outside," says manager Griffin Bufkin. "It's an old garage, kind of a dive really." There's one owner, Danny Camp, and two employees, Bufkin and bartender Martin, who hails from England via Austin, Texas. "We're thinking of getting a waitress," deadpans Bufkin.

The preferred drink, incidentally, is the Nazi-killer (100 proof Schnapps and Jaegermeister).

Lodged in the Deep South, Danny's is a perfect spot to politely ask the unforgiving, "How far is yonder?"

The Boot Hill Saloon, Daytona Beach, Florida.

If you're born to be wild, like a true nature's child, park your Harley at the Boot Hill Saloon and head in for a beer. Since 1973, the Boot Hill has been a fixture in the heart of transient Daytona Beach. Bikers, race fans, adventure-seekers, and locals all call the place home. At certain times of the year, hundreds of chromed invaders neatly park in shining rows ready to roar to life in Brando-like fashion. It's enough to warm the hearts of law-enforcement officers everywhere.

The decor is authentic honky-tonk with cement floors, pool tables, graffiti walls and blaring jukes. Tobacco-sullied lingerie, lacy undies, nylons and bras of all shapes and sizes dangle from the ceiling like so much laundry hung out

to dry. Each garment has a story. As Willie the bartender explains, "Nothing goes up unless they take it off in here first."

Regular patrons admit that there are fights from time to time, but usually it's just some "ass" causing trouble, and remember that every great tattoo tells a great story. Just ask the bar girl with the palm tree on her butt. She'll show you.

Believe it.

One word of warning. Don't venture into the cemetery across the street after dark. As the Boot Hill Saloon says on its award-winning matchbook: "Order a drink and have a seat. You're better off here than across the street."

Sebastian Beach Inn, Melbourne Beach, Florida.

The world's best beach bar at which to watch rockets being launched into space, this is an admittedly "super cruddy" place. It's famous for two things: great music, and the patrons who sign the walls after downing the requisite number of "Bahama Mama" drinks.

SBI reflects a burgeoning Central Florida music scene and has hosted the Screaming Iguanas of Love, Orlando's Fifth Column, and the hardcore hometown beach crowd fave, Brave New Tribe, with their danceable surf anthem, "Down to the Bottom." The bar even headlines country music acts such as Tennessee Jeanie. "When she sings, all the neighborhood dogs start cryin'," says one local.

The Tiki Bar, Key West, Florida.

Head to Key West and anyone with a lick of sense will direct you to the Tiki Bar, which is a certified Florida attraction. Halfway between Homestead and Key West, this oasis is a lovely liquid magnet on the seemingly endless causeway connecting Key West to the rest of the world.

by Ken **McKnight**

To stave off the maddening tropical heat, order the "original Rum Runner"—151 Rum, Blackberry Brandy, Banana Liqueur, grenadine, and frozen lime juice, which will surely freeze your head.

Park across the street and take the mini bus to the main entrance. The decor is palm-front tropics. Check your hard shoes and fishing poles at the front door, and enjoy the company of all those people you have passed or been passed up by on the highway.

Hussongs, Ensenada, Mexico.

Steve Bartlotti's "Tales of Hussongs," (B.C. issue 5) summed up the Mexican Beach bar best.

"Many a rambling Baja tale started with the preamble ...then we stopped at Hussongs," with a queer time machine where years wash away and suddenly you're 20 and drunk again."

Hussongs is world famous for two things: allowing you to get twisted with complete strangers, and encouraging patrons to try to hold on for 60 seconds to the shock box, which is two metal handles attached by wires to a car battery. The hollowed halls hold a legacy of gringo debauchery that spans 100 years—more than one person has lost virtue and lunch within its bluming confines.

Hussongs is a rite of passage for all SoCal college brats. And it may be the only bar in North America where you can yell "Fuck" and nobody listens. The penalty for not getting drunk at Hussongs? Having to walk into the toilet area without any shoes on.

Carlos O'Brien's, Puerta Vallarta, Mexico.

A Mexican fable, set in the darkest heart of the historic Mexican coast, Puerta Vallarta is a lit-up tourist town of impeccable clarity that invites anyone with $299 to visit, throw providence to the wind, and party!

Located smack in the middle of town with a gorgeous view of the bay, especially under a full moon, Carlos O'Brien's starts out romantic, but usually ends up featuring Manachi stomp fests. This may be because the tropical heat keeps you grabbing at your throat to quench the thirst.

Guzzle the beer if you wish but be careful just to sip the clear tequila. One friend was so inebriated on the cactus juice that he believed us when we later told him he had dropped his drawers while table-dancing until the local police intervened. Three days later, we coerced him into returning to Carlos O'Brien's. There, to our surprise, a young lovely asked him if she hadn't seen him the other night. If Carlos O'Brien's isn't enough for you, cross the street to the beach and parasail for five bucks behind 300 feet of rope driven by a crazy Mexican with a captain's hat on (he's one of the bartenders at Carlos O'Brien's).

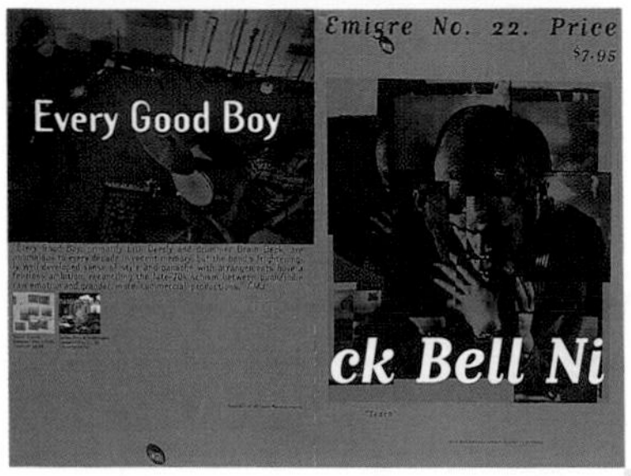

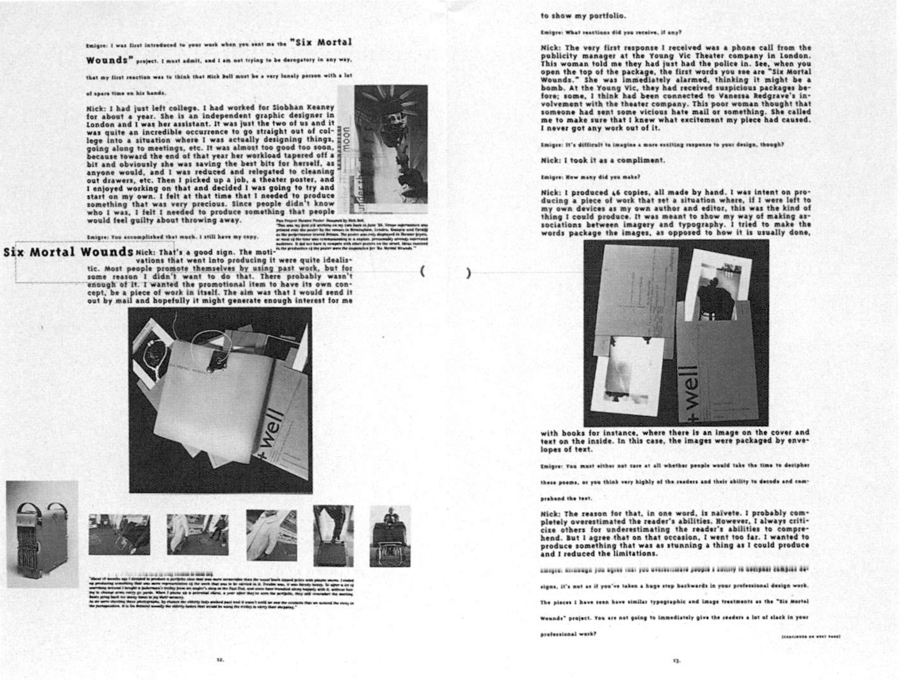

Emigre: I was first introduced to your work when you sent me the "Six Mortal Wounds" project. I must admit, and I am not trying to be derogatory in any way, that my first reaction was to think that Nick Bell must be a very lonely person with a lot of spare time on his hands.

Nick: I had just left college. I had worked for Siobhan Keaney for about a year. She is an independent graphic designer in London and I was her assistant. It was just the two of us and it was quite an incredible occurrence to go straight out of college into a situation where I was actually designing things, going along to meetings, etc. It was almost too good too soon, because toward the end of that year her workload tapered off a bit and obviously she was saving the best bits for herself, as anyone would, and I was reduced and relegated to cleaning out drawers, etc. Then I picked up a job, a theater poster, and I enjoyed working on that and decided I was going to try and start on my own. I felt at that time that I needed to produce something that was very precious. Since people didn't know who I was, I felt I needed to produce something that people would feel guilty about throwing away.

Emigre: You accomplished that much. I still have my copy.

Six Mortal Wounds

Nick: That's a good sign. The motivations that went into producing it were quite idealistic. Most people promote themselves by using past work, but for some reason I didn't want to do that. There probably wasn't enough of it. I wanted the promotional item to have its own concept, be a piece of work in itself. The aim was that I would send it out by mail and hopefully it might generate enough interest for me to show my portfolio.

Emigre: What reactions did you receive, if any?

Nick: The very first response I received was a phone call from the publicity manager at the Young Vic Theater company in London. This woman told me they had just had the police in. See, when you open the top of the package, the first words you see are "Six Mortal Wounds." She was immediately alarmed, thinking it might be a bomb. At the Young Vic, they had received suspicious packages before; some, I think had been connected to Vanessa Redgrave's involvement with the theater company. This poor woman thought that someone had sent some vicious hate mail or something. She called me to make sure that I knew what excitement my piece had caused. I never got any work out of it.

Emigre: It's difficult to imagine a more exciting response to your design, though?

Nick: I took it as a compliment.

Emigre: How many did you make?

Nick: I produced 46 copies, all made by hand. I was intent on producing a piece of work that set a situation where, if I were left to my own devices as my own author and editor, this was the kind of thing I could produce. It was meant to show my way of making associations between imagery and typography. I tried to make the words package the images, as opposed to how it is usually done, with books for instance, where there is an image on the cover and text on the inside. In this case, the images were packaged by envelopes of text.

Emigre: You must either not care at all whether people would take the time to decipher these poems, or you think very highly of the readers and their ability to decode and comprehend the text.

Nick: The reason for that, in one word, is naïvete. I probably completely overestimated the reader's abilities. However, I always criticize others for underestimating the reader's abilities to comprehend. But I agree that on that occasion, I went too far. I wanted to produce something that was as stunning a thing as I could produce and I reduced the limitations.

Emigre: Although you agree that you overestimate people's ability to decipher complex designs, it's not as if you've taken a huge step backwards in your professional design work. The pieces I have seen have similar typographic and image treatments as the "Six Mortal Wounds" project. You are not going to immediately give the readers a lot of slack in your professional work?

(continued on next page)

12.

13.

Magazine 雑誌
"Emigre" #22 USA 1992
AD,D:Rudy Vanderlans P:Andy Rumball
DF:Emigre CL:Emigre

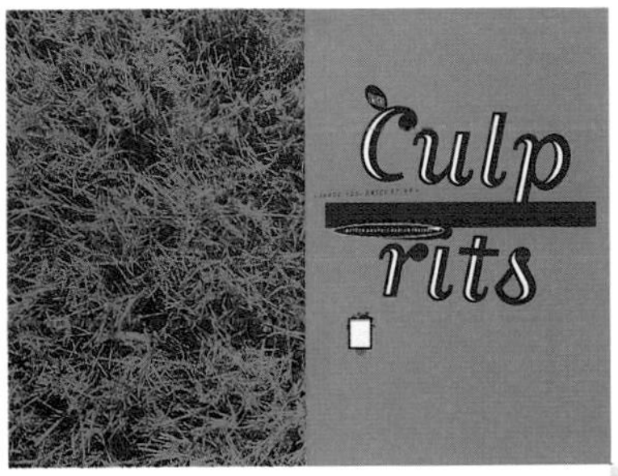

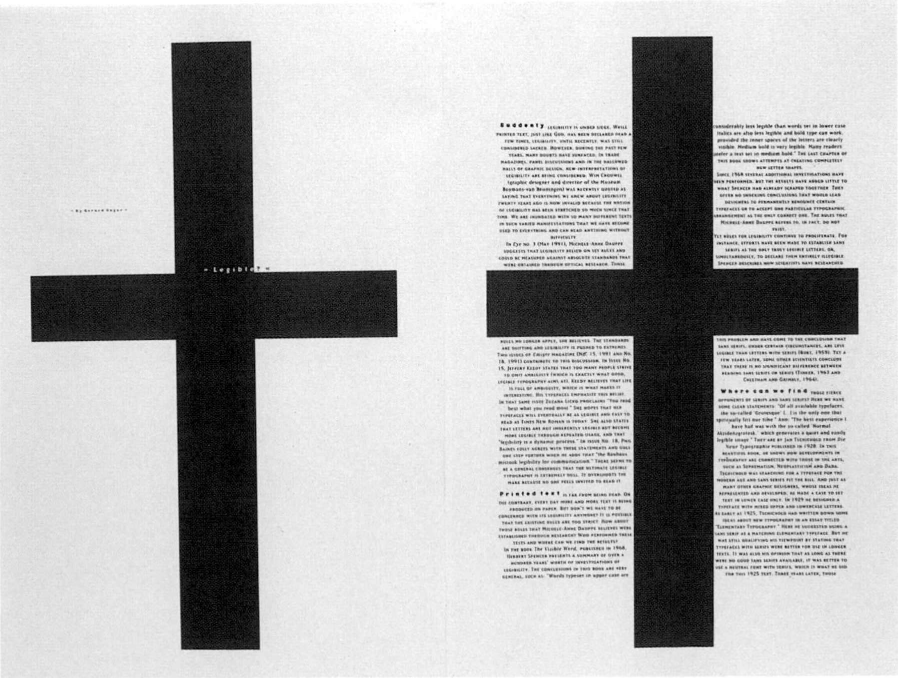

Magazine 雑誌
"Emigre" #23 USA 1992
AD,D,P:Rudy Vanderlans DF:Emigre
CL:Emigre

Magazine 誌

"Emigre" #24   USA 1992

AD,D,P:Rudy Vanderlans   DF:Emigre

CL:Emigre

neo-
mania

N. 24

History is no longer 5, 10, 15 years ago...

functional, and socially responsible. While these values had
their merit, they can at times limit the discussion. In the
recent AIGA *Journal* on Modernism,¹ Kathy McCoy, Da
Friedman, and Massimo Vignelli, in spite of their differing
viewpoints, all make note of the disparity between the com
plexity and richness of the original Modernist ideologies and
what has become merely an applied Modernist style.

Yet the real contradiction lies between stripped-down Modernist precepts
in theory and that which the profession values *in practice*, where formal
novelty is most frequently rewarded, and each new fashion is consumed
and spent overnight. As our ideals wither in the face of this dilemma,
style itself becomes the scapegoat and the discussion grinds to a halt.

If orm follows fashion
WOLFGANG WEINGART PARTICIPATED in the revo
against the strict minimalist approach of his Swiss
predecessors. While his work is considered within
the Modernist idiom, his experimentation with form
and structure rejected the "neutral envelope" approach
ostensibly objective form-making in favor of intuitive choices
and personal expression. When visiting CalArts in 199
Weingart commented with disdain that he was no longer in
fashion, as though whatever had replaced him as the current
design-of-choice was merely a trend somehow not as worth
as the trend he once embodied. Did he mean that the visual
expression of his ideas had lost its power to communicate as
time had altered its context? Or were the ideas themselves no
longer popular? Or was it just that designers had seen the
style of his work for too long and now looked to something
new, out of boredom alone? I asked Weingart if he could elab
orate on what appears to be a preoccupation with form
fashion' (style) within the graphic design profession. What
is this affliction that makes graphic designer
crave perpetual stylistic (r)evolution? Weingart
evaded the question, inhibiting inquiry into a realm that
makes most designers uneasy.

THAT WHICH WE CALL TYPOGRAPHIC
STYLE IS FIRST AND FOREMOST
DETERMINED BY OUR WAY OF LIFE
AND OUR WORKING CONDITIONS.
— Jan Tschichold, On Typography, 1952

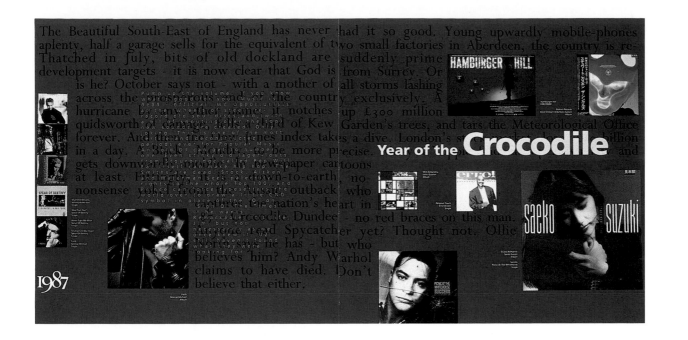

Brochure Spreads ブローシュアページ

Celebration UK 1991
AD,D:Rob O'Connor D:Rob Mills
DF:Stylorouge CL:Stylorouge

Magazine Spread 雑誌ページ
"i-D Magazine" Issue 90 March 1991 UK 1991
AD:Stephen Male D:Omaid Hiwaizi
P:Matthew R. Lewis DF:Nice CL:i-D Magazine

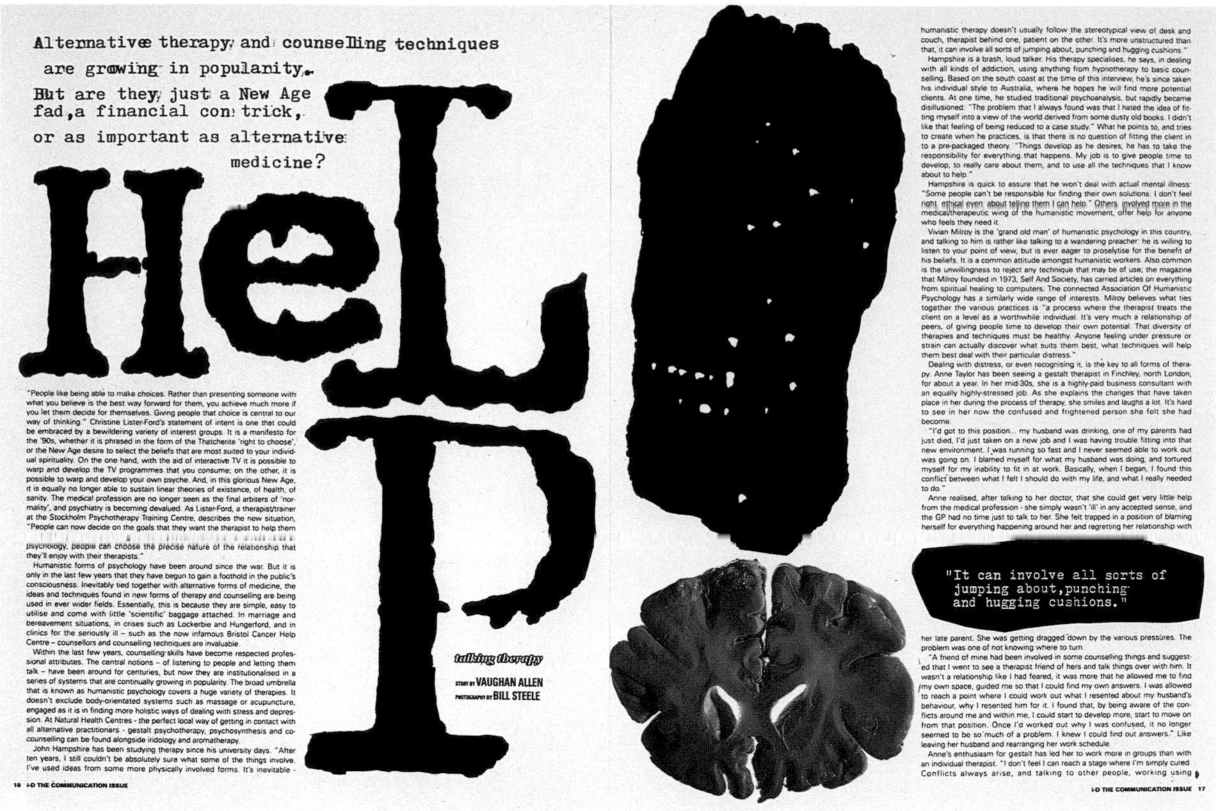

Alternative therapy and counselling techniques are growing in popularity. But are they just a New Age fad, a financial con trick, or as important as alternative medicine?

HeLP

talking therapy

STORY BY VAUGHAN ALLEN
PHOTOGRAPHY BY BILL STEELE

"People like being able to make choices. Rather than presenting someone with what you believe is the best way forward for them, you achieve much more if you let them decide for themselves. Giving people that choice is central to our way of thinking." Christine Lister-Ford's statement of intent is one that could be embraced by a bewildering variety of interest groups. It is a manifesto for the '90s, whether it is phrased in the form of the Thatcherite 'right to choose', or the New Age desire to select the beliefs that are most suited to your individual spirituality. On the one hand, with the aid of interactive TV it is possible to warp and develop the TV programmes that you consume; on the other, it is possible to warp and develop your own psyche. And, in this glorious New Age, it is equally no longer able to sustain linear theories of existence, of health, of sanity. The medical profession are no longer seen as the final arbiters of 'normality', and psychiatry is becoming devalued. As Lister-Ford, a therapist/trainer at the Stockholm Psychotherapy Training Centre, describes the new situation, "People can now decide on the goals that they want the therapist to help them [illegible] psychology, people can choose the precise nature of the relationship that they'll enjoy with their therapists."

Humanistic forms of psychology have been around since the war. But it is only in the last few years that they have begun to gain a foothold in the public's consciousness. Inevitably tied together with alternative forms of medicine, the ideas and techniques found in new forms of therapy and counselling are being used in ever wider fields. Essentially, this is because they are simple, easy to utilise and come with little 'scientific' baggage attached. In marriage and bereavement situations, in crises such as Lockerbie and Hungerford, and in clinics for the seriously ill – such as the now infamous Bristol Cancer Help Centre – counsellors and counselling techniques are invaluable.

Within the last few years, counselling skills have become respected professional attributes. The central notions – of listening to people and letting them talk – have been around for centuries, but now they are institutionalised in a series of systems that are continually growing in popularity. The broad umbrella that is known as humanistic psychology covers a huge variety of therapies. It doesn't exclude body-orientated systems such as massage or acupuncture, engaged as it is in finding more holistic ways of dealing with stress and depression. At Natural Health Centres - the perfect local way of getting in contact with all alternative practitioners - gestalt psychotherapy, psychosynthesis and co-counselling can be found alongside iridology and aromatherapy.

John Hampshire has been studying therapy since his university days. "After ten years, I still couldn't be absolutely sure what some of the things involve. I've used ideas from some more physically involved forms. It's inevitable - humanistic therapy doesn't usually follow the stereotypical view of desk and couch, therapist behind one, patient on the other. It's more unstructured than that, it can involve all sorts of jumping about, punching and hugging cushions."

Hampshire is a brash, loud talker. His therapy specialises, he says, in dealing with all kinds of addiction, using anything from hypnotherapy to basic counselling. Based on the south coast at the time of this interview, he's since taken his individual style to Australia, where he hopes he will find more potential clients. At one time, he studied traditional psychoanalysis, but rapidly became disillusioned: "The problem that I always found was that I hated the idea of fitting myself into a view of the world derived from some dusty old books. I didn't like that feeling of being reduced to a case study." What he points to, and tries to create when he practices, is that there is no question of fitting the client in to a pre-packaged theory. "Things develop as he desires; he has to take the responsibility for everything that happens. My job is to give people time to develop, to really care about them, and to use all the techniques that I know about to help."

Hampshire is quick to assure that he won't deal with actual mental illness: "Some people can't be responsible for finding their own solutions. I don't feel right, ethical even, about telling them I can help." Others, involved more in the medical/therapeutic wing of the humanistic movement, offer help for anyone who feels they need it.

Vivian Milroy is the 'grand old man' of humanistic psychology in this country, and talking to him is rather like talking to a wandering preacher: he is willing to listen to your point of view, but is ever eager to proselytise for the benefit of his beliefs. It is a common attitude amongst humanistic workers. Also common is the unwillingness to reject any technique that may be of use; the magazine that Milroy founded in 1973, Self And Society, has carried articles on everything from spiritual healing to computers. The connected Association Of Humanistic Psychology has a similarly wide range of interests. Milroy believes what ties together the various practices is "a process where the therapist treats the client on a level as a worthwhile individual. It's very much a relationship of peers, of giving people time to develop their own potential. That diversity of therapies and techniques must be healthy. Anyone feeling under pressure or strain can actually discover what suits them best, what techniques will help them best deal with their particular distress."

Dealing with distress, or even recognising it, is the key to all forms of therapy. Anne Taylor has been seeing a gestalt therapist in Finchley, north London, for about a year. In her mid-30s, she is a highly-paid business consultant with an equally highly-stressed job. As she explains the changes that have taken place in her during the process of therapy, she smiles and laughs a lot. It's hard to see in her now the confused and frightened person she felt she had become.

"I'd got to this position... my husband was drinking, one of my parents had just died, I'd just taken on a new job and I was having trouble fitting into that new environment. I was running so fast and I never seemed able to work out was going on. I blamed myself for what my husband was doing, and tortured myself for my inability to fit in at work. Basically, when I began, I found this conflict between what I felt I should do with my life, and what I really needed to do."

Anne realised, after talking to her doctor, that she could get very little help from the medical profession - she simply wasn't 'ill' in any accepted sense, and the GP had no time just to talk to her. She felt trapped in a position of blaming herself for everything happening around her and regretting her relationship with

"It can involve all sorts of jumping about, punching and hugging cushions."

her late parent. She was getting dragged down by the various pressures. The problem was one of not knowing where to turn.

"A friend of mine had been involved in some counselling things and suggested that I went to see a therapist friend of hers and talk things over with him. It wasn't a relationship like I had feared, it was more that he allowed me to find my own space, guided me so that I could find my own answers. I was allowed to reach a point where I could work out what I resented about my husband's behaviour, why I resented him for it. I found that, by being aware of the conflicts around me and within me, I could start to develop more, start to move on from that position. Once I'd worked out why I was confused, it no longer seemed to be so much of a problem. I knew I could find out answers." Like leaving her husband and rearranging her work schedule.

Anne's enthusiasm for gestalt has led her to work more in groups than with an individual therapist. "I don't feel I can reach a stage where I'm simply cured. Conflicts always arise, and talking to other people, working using ▶

16 I-D THE COMMUNICATION ISSUE

I-D THE COMMUNICATION ISSUE 17

Magazine Spread 雑誌ページ
"i-D Magazine" Issue 89 February 91 UK 1991
AD:Stephen Male D:Omaid Hiwaizi P:Bill Steele
DF:Nice CL:i-D Magazine

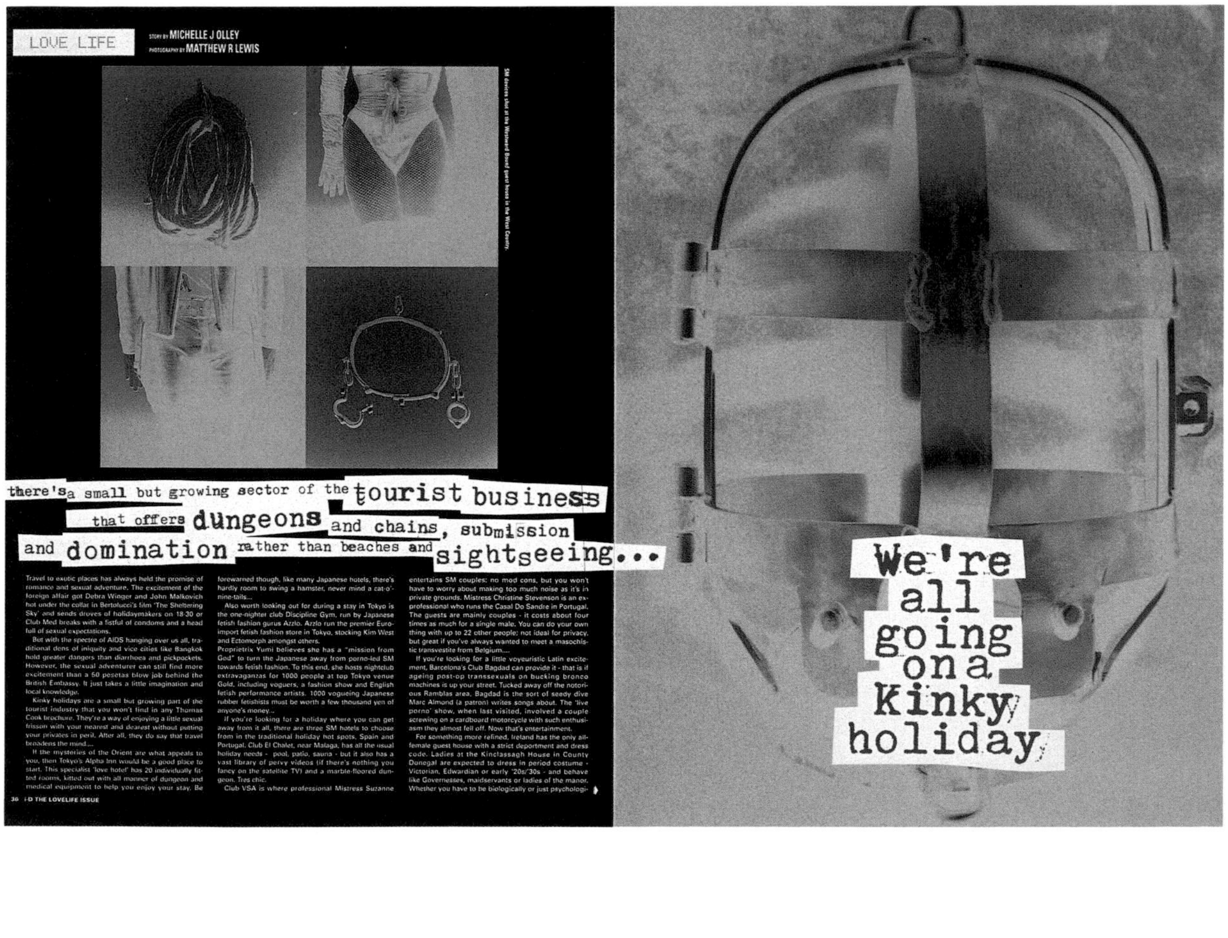

LOVE LIFE

STORY BY MICHELLE J OLLEY
PHOTOGRAPHY BY MATTHEW R LEWIS

SM devices shot at the Westward Bound guest house in the West Country.

there's a small but growing sector of the tourist business that offers dungeons and chains, submission and domination rather than beaches and sightseeing...

Travel to exotic places has always held the promise of romance and sexual adventure. The excitement of the foreign affair got Debra Winger and John Malkovich hot under the collar in Bertolucci's film 'The Sheltering Sky' and sends droves of holidaymakers on 18-30 or Club Med breaks with a fistful of condoms and a head full of sexual expectations.

But with the spectre of AIDS hanging over us all, traditional dens of iniquity and vice cities like Bangkok hold greater dangers than diarrhoea and pickpockets. However, the sexual adventurer can still find more excitement than a 50 pesetas blow job behind the British Embassy. It just takes a little imagination and local knowledge.

Kinky holidays are a small but growing part of the tourist industry that you won't find in any Thomas Cook brochure. They're a way of enjoying a little sexual frisson with your nearest and dearest without putting your privates in peril. After all, they do say that travel broadens the mind....

If the mysteries of the Orient are what appeals to you, then Tokyo's Alpha Inn would be a good place to start. This specialist 'love hotel' has 20 individually fitted rooms, kitted out with all manner of dungeon and medical equipment to help you enjoy your stay. Be forewarned though, like many Japanese hotels, there's hardly room to swing a hamster, never mind a cat-o'-nine-tails...

Also worth looking out for during a stay in Tokyo is the one-nighter club Discipline Gym, run by Japanese fetish fashion gurus Azzlo. Azzlo run the premier Euro-import fetish fashion store in Tokyo, stocking Kim West and Ectomorph amongst others.
Proprietrix Yumi believes she has a "mission from God" to turn the Japanese away from porno-led SM towards fetish fashion. To this end, she hosts nightclub extravaganzas for 1000 people at top Tokyo venue Gold, including voguers, a fashion show and English fetish performance artists. 1000 vogueing Japanese rubber fetishists must be worth a few thousand yen of anyone's money...

If you're looking for a holiday where you can get away from it all, there are three SM hotels to choose from in the traditional holiday hot spots, Spain and Portugal. Club El Chalet, near Malaga, has all the usual holiday needs - pool, patio, sauna - but it also has a vast library of pervy videos (if there's nothing you fancy on the satellite TV) and a marble-floored dungeon. Tres chic.

Club VSA is where professional Mistress Suzanne entertains SM couples: no mod cons, but you won't have to worry about making too much noise as it's in private grounds. Mistress Christine Stevenson is an ex-professional who runs the Casal Do Sandre in Portugal. The guests are mainly couples - it costs about four times as much for a single male. You can do your own thing with up to 22 other people: not ideal for privacy, but great if you've always wanted to meet a masochistic transvestite from Belgium....

If you're looking for a little voyeuristic Latin excitement, Barcelona's Club Bagdad can provide it - that is if ageing post-op transsexuals on bucking bronco machines is up your street. Tucked away off the notorious Ramblas area, Bagdad is the sort of seedy dive Marc Almond (a patron) writes songs about. The 'live porno' show, when last visited, involved a couple screwing on a cardboard motorcycle with such enthusiasm they almost fell off. Now that's entertainment.

For something more refined, Ireland has the only all-female guest house with a strict deportment and dress code. Ladies at the Kinclassagh House in County Donegal are expected to dress in period costume - Victorian, Edwardian or early '20s/'30s - and behave like Governesses, maidservants or ladies of the manor. Whether you have to be biologically or just psychologi- ▶

36 I-D THE LOVELIFE ISSUE

We're all going on a Kinky holiday

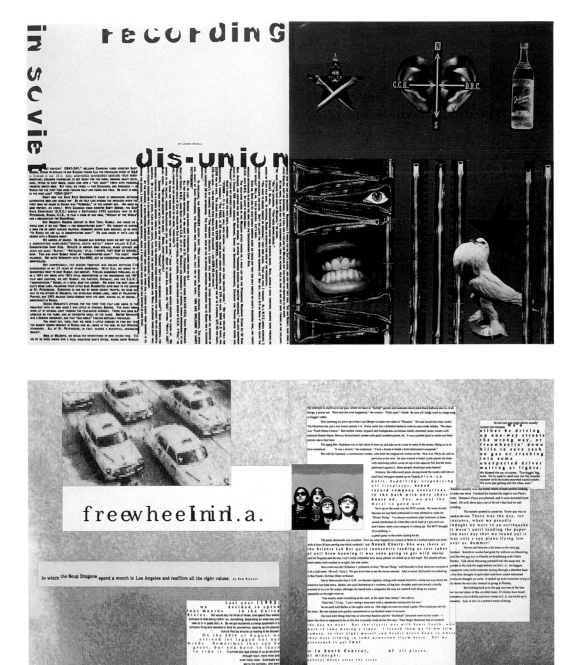

Magazine 雑誌

"Ray Gun" March '93   USA 1993

AD:David Carson   D:Joe Polevy   P:Anthony Artiaga

I:Amy Guip   DF:David Carson Design   CL:Ray Gun Magazine

Magazine 雑誌

"Ray Gun" Feb '93   USA 1993

AD,D:David Carson   P:Mike Hassler, David Hawkes, Mike Bloom, Steve Stickler

I:Doug Aitken   DF:David Carson Design   CL:Ray Gun Magazine

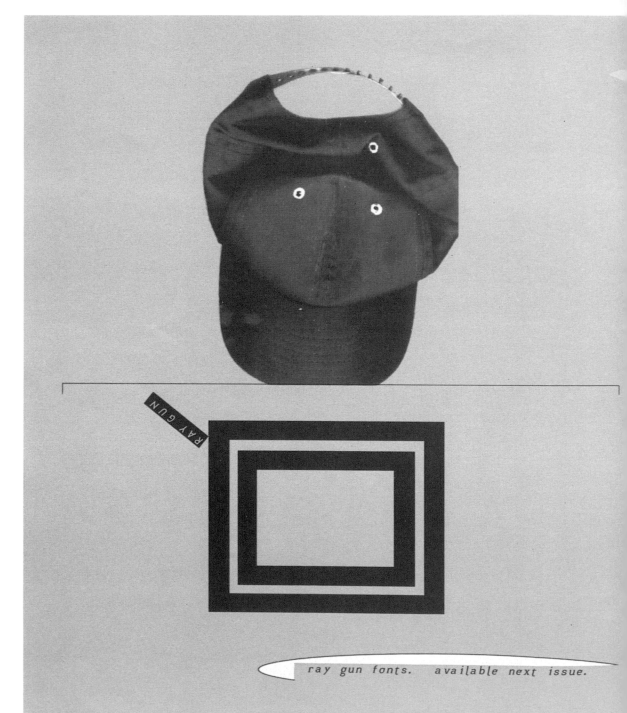

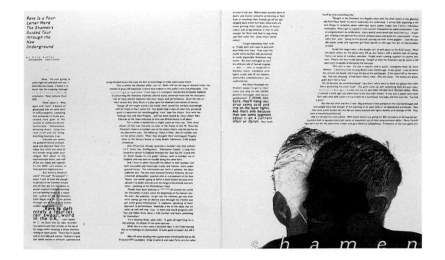

Rave Is a Four-
Letter Word
The Shamen's
Guided Tour
through the
New
Underground

by Erin Culley
photographs: Joyce Culver

s h a m e n

---

flaming

flaming

"It's a depressed, poverty-stricken city. Most of the people don't have jobs. There's nothing to
money to do it with," says Wayne Coyne, singer/guitarist, speaking about the band's
, Oklahoma City.
"There are worse places to live," offers bassist Mike Ivins.
Perhaps it was the "lack of anything else to do" there that inspired the Flaming Lips' initial
and their debut self-titled EP, released on their own Lovely Sorts of Death Records.
Done using Coyne's father's "barter system," they thought they would make the record, and that would "be about it.
There was no plan going into it."
Eight years and five albums later, the current incarnation of the Lips, including drummer Steven and guitarist
Ron (both of whom dislike their last names), are sitting in the dressing room of the Whiskey A Go-Go in a circle of
folding chairs. Tonight's headlining performance will mark their first L.A. gig in support of their major label debut,
Hit to Death in the Future Head.
"It doesn't really feel like, 'Welcome to the Corporate World,'" says Coyne in regard to their Warner Bros. signing. "It's just
more organized. When they signed us, we never got the idea that they thought, 'Okay, you guys go make the perfect record and sell
10 million copies.' They just want us to make Flaming Lips records. If our next record sounds like we've sold out, it would be
because of us."This release did get them their first Parental Advisory label. Even if the only so-called "explicit lyric" on the album
is within the grooves of "Felt Good to Burn": "We just slept and fucked and not high."
"I think it was the 'fucked' that did it," he continues. "You can say 'fuck' but you can't mean fucking. It's fine to say
'fuck off.' You just can't mean that unspeakable deed. To me, the label looks stupid in the corner (of the CD jacket). The only argument I
heard for it was that someone like Wal-Mart wouldn't carry it. But most people who buy our records don't go in there anyway. They
wouldn't carry Nevermind either. Or didn't they put a sticker over his dick?"
"I saw the Guns n' Roses record there," injects Ivins.
"They'll sell anything if they think they can make money off it," says Coyne.
Recorded in two different studios in New York in 1991, Hit to Death was supposed to be released on St. Patrick's Day (March 17, 1992), but Biz Markie
fouled up the plan.
"Around Christmas '91, the Biz Markie sampling suit went down," explains Coyne. In it, singer Gilbert O'Sullivan successfully sued the Biz for
his blatant sample of "Alone Again Naturally." "That really fucked Warner Brothers up. Anything that had a sample on it had to get approved, and we
had used this Michael Kamen Brazil sample. The record had been done for six months, and no one cared unti the suit. The sample was from the movie,
and movie people don't really care if a record company needs their stuff. So the approval took a long time."
More than a year after its completion, an agreement was reached and the album was released. Produced by the Lips
and Dave Fridmann, the album shows that the Lips remain completely unaffected, creating garage-pop-thrash
psychedelia with genuine wit and a sense of experimentation. (There's that unlistenable, unlisted 30 minute track...)
Over the years, the Lips have undergone several personnel changes. In the beginning, Coyne's brother,
Mark, was the lead vocalist. But he quit shortly after the first EP, and now, "works for Dad. He owns a house. He
mows the lawn. It just wasn't his thing."
Reduced to a three-piece band, they attracted the attention of L.A.'s independent Restless Records. Three records
later, drummer Richard English left. On their fourth album, In a Priest Driven Ambulance, they became a foursome
again, adding second guitarist Jonathan Donahue and drummer Nathan Roberts. Both perform on Hit to Death but
left prior to the album's release. Donahue now concentrates on his band, Mercury Rev, while Roberts "married an
evil woman and lost his desire."
Bassist Ivins has been with the group since day one, despite nearly being electricuted by the
bubble machine during a couple of live performances. The current line-up plans on recording soon.
"It's not like we have any other options," says Coyne. "This is what we do. We can't go back to school. There's nothing else
er we do this, or we do nothing."

flaming

flaming

Brochure Spreads ブローシュアページ

How Design Conference USA 1992

AD,D:Carlos Segura　P:Photonica

CW:Bruce Charles & How　DF:Segura　CL:How Magazine

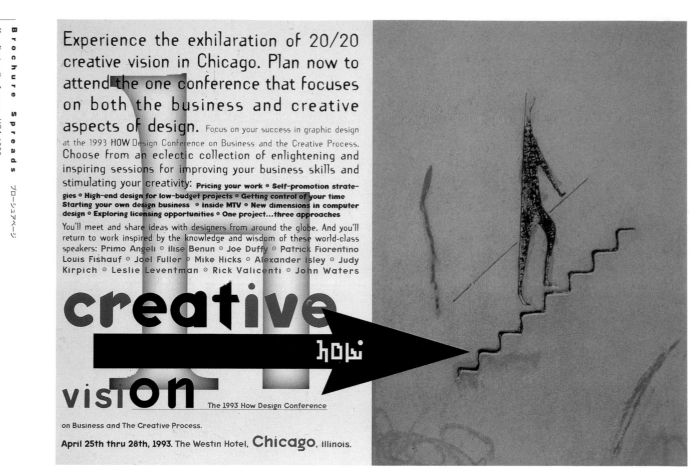

Experience the exhilaration of 20/20 creative vision in Chicago. Plan now to attend the one conference that focuses on both the business and creative aspects of design. Focus on your success in graphic design at the 1993 HOW Design Conference on Business and the Creative Process. Choose from an eclectic collection of enlightening and inspiring sessions for improving your business skills and stimulating your creativity: **Pricing your work ○ Self-promotion strategies ○ High-end design for low-budget projects ○ Getting control of your time Starting your own design business ○ inside MTV ○ New dimensions in computer design ○ Exploring licensing opportunities ○ One project...three approaches**

You'll meet and share ideas with designers from around the globe. And you'll return to work inspired by the knowledge and wisdom of these world-class speakers: Primo Angeli ○ Ilise Benun ○ Joe Duffy ○ Patrick Fiorentino Louis Fishauf ○ Joel Fuller ○ Mike Hicks ○ Alexander Isley ○ Judy Kirpich ○ Leslie Leventman ○ Rick Valicenti ○ John Waters

creative
vision

how

The 1993 How Design Conference on Business and The Creative Process.

April 25th thru 28th, 1993. The Westin Hotel, **Chicago**, Illinois.

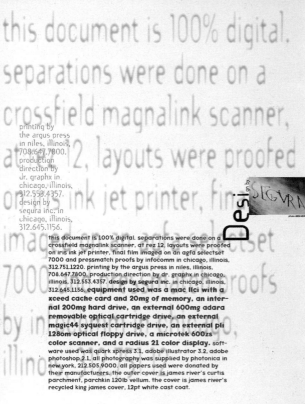

this document is 100% digital. separations were done on a crossfield magnalink scanner, at rez 12, layouts were proofed on iris ink jet printer, fir...

printing by the argus press in niles, illinois, 708.647.7800. production direction by dr. graphx in chicago, illinois, 312.553.4357. design by segura inc. in chicago, illinois, 312.645.1156.

Desi on by SEGURA

this document is 100% digital. separations were done on a crossfield magnalink scanner, at rez 12, layouts were proofed on iris ink jet printer, final film imaged on an agfa selectset 7000 and pressmatch proofs by infocomm in chicago, illinois, 312.751.1220. printing by the argus press in niles, illinois, 708.647.7800. production direction by dr. graphx in chicago, illinois, 312.553.4357. design by segura inc. in chicago, illinois, 312.645.1156. **equipment used was a mac IIci with a xceed cache card and 20mg of memory, an internal 200mg hard drive, an external 600mg adara removable optical cartridge drive, an external magic44 syquest cartridge drive, an external pli 128om optical floppy drive, a microtek 600zs color scanner, and a radius 21 color display.** software used was quark xpress 3.1, adobe illustrator 3.2, adobe photoshop 2.1, all photography was supplied by photonica in new york, 212.505.9000. all papers used were donated by their manufacturers. the outer cover is james river's curtis parchment, parchkin 120lb vellum. the cover is james river's recycled king james cover, 12pt white cast coat.

Brochure ブローシュア

Neocon 92 USA 1992

AD,D:Carlos Segura P:Geof Kern CW:Alan Gandelman

DF:Segura CL:The Merchandise Mart

NeoCon92 proudly thanks the many indusTRY professionals, advisors, and organizations who have helped make this year's event a TRUE marketplace of ideas and innovative THINKing.

Furnish Your Mind

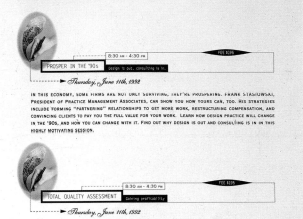

PROSPER IN THE '90s 8:30 AM - 4:30 PM Design is out, consulting is in. FEE $195

▶ *Thursday, June 11th, 1992*

IN THIS ECONOMY, SOME FIRMS ARE NOT ONLY SURVIVING, THEY'RE PROSPERING. FRANK STASIOWSKI, PRESIDENT OF PRACTICE MANAGEMENT ASSOCIATES, CAN SHOW YOU HOW YOURS CAN, TOO. HIS STRATEGIES INCLUDE FORMING "PARTNERING" RELATIONSHIPS TO GET MORE WORK, RESTRUCTURING COMPENSATION, AND CONVINCING CLIENTS TO PAY YOU THE FULL VALUE FOR YOUR WORK. LEARN HOW DESIGN PRACTICE WILL CHANGE IN THE '90S, AND HOW YOU CAN CHANGE WITH IT. FIND OUT WHY DESIGN IS OUT AND CONSULTING IS IN IN THIS HIGHLY MOTIVATING SESSION.

TOTAL QUALITY ASSESSMENT 8:30 AM - 4:30 PM Gaining profitability FEE $195

▶ *Thursday, June 11th, 1992*

LEARN HOW THE QUALITY MOVEMENT CAN LEAD YOUR COMPANY TO PROFITABILITY AND RESULTS. DR. RAYMOND ARO, A HIGHLY EXPERIENCED PRODUCTIVITY AND WORKPLACE CLIMATE SPECIALIST, WILL DEMONSTRATE THE REAL ISSUES IN THE QUALITY MOVEMENT, AND GIVE YOU THE STANDARDS AND GUIDELINES FOR IMPLEMENTATION. IN THIS INTERACTIVE SESSION, HE WILL PRESENT A QUALITY SYSTEM SELF-ASSESSMENT YOU CAN APPLY TO YOUR OWN COMPANY, AND PUT THE ENTIRE PROCESS IN PERSPECTIVE.

INTERIOR ENVIRONMENTS 8:30 AM -12:00 PM & 1:00 PM -6:00 PM Challenges for the 90's FEES

▶ *Thursday, June 11th, 1992*

THE COUNCIL OF FEDERAL INTERIOR DESIGNERS AND THE INSTITUTE OF BUSINESS DESIGNERS TEAM UP FOR THE FIRST TIME TO OFFER THIS COURSE TO PROVIDE YOU WITH UP-TO-DATE INFORMATION TO ASSIST YOU IN YOUR DAILY PERFORMANCE. THE DAY WILL BEGIN WITH A GENERAL BUSINESS MEETING AND A DISCUSSION ON DESIGN PROFESSION UNIFICATION. THE AFTERNOON SESSION ADDRESSES INTERIOR ENVIRONMENTAL ISSUES RELATED TO THE AMERICANS WITH DISABILITIES ACT. THE AFTERNOON SESSION AWARDS .5 CEU CREDIT.

FEES: MEMBERS $95, NON-MEMBERS $145. AFTERNOON ONLY: MEMBERS $50, NON-MEMBERS $75

PRE AND POST **NeoCon92** SEMINARS.

WE BEGIN WITH A HAND-PICKED TEAM OF ART CENTER FACULTY AND ALUMNI WITH

HOW DOES ACCESS WORK?

Brochure Spread　ブローシュアページ

Art Center Access　USA 1992

AD:Rebeca Mendez　D:Darren Namaye　P:Steven A. Heller

DF:Art Center College of Design, Design Office　CL:Art Center College of Design

Graphic and Packaging Design

Graphic designers are communications specialists. Whether they are creating printed material, signage, video graphics, or computer imagery, their objective is to inform. And their language—with its vocabulary of color, symbols, type, and images—is truly global. Attaining fluency in that language is only one of the goals of graphic and packaging design majors at Art Center; students learn to be researchers, analysts, and organizers as well as graphic artists.

"Our assignment was to present the periodic table of elements in a new way and to illustrate five of the elements in the poster. Other students selected individual images, like a cow for calcium, but I tried to find one picture that contained all five. I looked through many books to find a train that had all the elements I needed. It also had to be moving from left to right to work in my composition. I placed the image of the train underneath my typography so that the C in atomic, for example, overlays the train's plume of smoke, which contains carbon. This was an excellent exercise in proportion, spatial relationships, typography, color, and texture."

Brochure Spread　ブローシュアページ

Art Center College of Design View　USA 1992

AD:Rebeca Mendez　D:Darren Namaye　P:Steven A. Heller (Principal Photography)

Editor:Karen Jacobson　DF:Art Center College of Design, Design Office　CL:Art Center College of Design

TO THE NEEDS OF THE MANUFACTURER. THESE TEAMS CAN PROVIDE

MANY SERVICES, INCLUDING:

■ DESIGN AUDITS: OUR CONSULTANTS WILL ANALYZE THE EFFEC-

TIVENESS OF YOUR COMPANY'S CURRENT DESIGN PRACTICES, PIN-

POINTING STRENGTHS AND IDENTIFYING PROBLEM AREAS. THE TEAM

WILL THEN MAKE CONCRETE RECOMMENDATIONS THAT CAN HELP

YOU IMPLEMENT A MORE EFFECTIVE DESIGN MANAGEMENT POLICY.

Photography

Photography doesn't merely record what is visible; it makes visible. Whether it is used for an advertising campaign or a personal project, the camera is a tool of communication, limited only by the user's imagination. Working with a faculty of professional photographers, Art Center students learn that it is the care and skill exercised before the exposure is made that distinguish great images from ordinary ones.

"The subject is a good friend of mine who had just shaved his head. I felt that this was the right moment to make a portrait. For some here in America nudity is an issue, but for me, a Brazilian, it is not; the face and body express equally. I chose the 4x5-inch format because of the relationship it forces between subject and photographer. It takes time to set lights, subject, and camera angle in the right positions. The process is slow and makes the subject forget the image he has of himself. This permits me to get closer and to meet him on a different level, one that may be unknown, even to myself."

Catalogue Spreads カタログページ

100 Show USA 1992
AD:Katherine McCoy D.P.:Mark Sylvester
DF:Cranbrook Academy of Art, Department of Design CL:American Center for Design

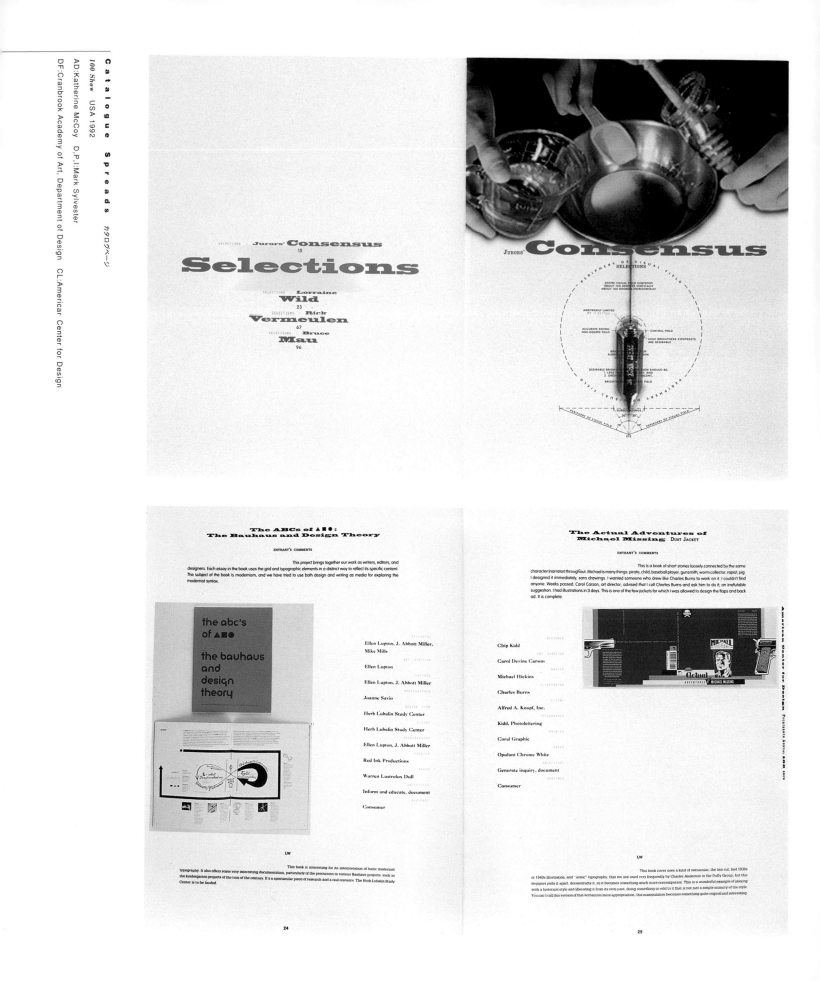

SELECTIONS | Jurors' **Consensus**
15
Selections
SELECTIONS | Lorraine
Wild
23
SUGGESTIONS | Rick
Vermeulen
67
SELECTIONS | Bruce
Mau
96

JURORS' **Consensus**
SELECTIONS

The ABCs of ▲■●:
The Bauhaus and Design Theory

ENTRANT'S COMMENTS

This project brings together our work as writers, editors, and designers. Each essay in the book uses the grid and typographic elements in a distinct way to reflect its specific content. The subject of the book is modernism, and we have tried to use both design and writing as media for exploring the modernist syntax.

the abc's
of ▲■●

the bauhaus
and
design
theory

DESIGNERS	Ellen Lupton, J. Abbott Miller, Mike Mills
ART DIRECTOR	Ellen Lupton
EDITORS	Ellen Lupton, J. Abbott Miller
PHOTOGRAPHER	Joanne Savio
DESIGN FIRM	Herb Lubalin Study Center
CLIENT	Herb Lubalin Study Center
TYPOGRAPHERS	Ellen Lupton, J. Abbott Miller
PRINTER	Red Ink Productions
PAPER	Warren Lustrolux Dull
OBJECTIVES	Inform and educate, document
AUDIENCE	Consumer

LW

This book is interesting for its interpretation of basic modernist typography. It also offers some very interesting documentation, particularly of the precursors to various Bauhaus projects, such as the kindergarten projects of the turn of the century. It's a spectacular piece of research and a real resource. The Herb Lubalin Study Center is to be lauded.

24

The Actual Adventures of
Michael Missing DUST JACKET

ENTRANT'S COMMENTS

This is a book of short stories loosely connected by the same character (narrator) throughout. Michael is many things: pirate, child, baseball player, gunsmith, worm collector, rapist, pig. I designed it immediately, sans drawings. I wanted someone who drew like Charles Burns to work on it. I couldn't find anyone. Weeks passed. Carol Carson, art director, advised that I call Charles Burns and ask him to do it, an irrefutable suggestion. I had illustrations in 3 days. This is one of the few jackets for which I was allowed to design the flaps and back ad. It is complete.

DESIGNER	Chip Kidd
ART DIRECTOR	Carol Devine Carson
WRITER	Michael Hickins
ILLUSTRATION	Charles Burns
CLIENT	Alfred A. Knopf, Inc.
TYPOGRAPHER	Kidd, Photolettering
PRINTER	Coral Graphic
PAPER	Opulant Chrome White
OBJECTIVES	Generate inquiry, document
AUDIENCE	Consumer

LW

This book cover uses a kind of vernacular, the line cut, bad 1930s or 1940s illustration, and "ironic" typography, that we see used very frequently by Charles Anderson or the Duffy Group, but this designer pulls it apart, deconstructs it, so it becomes something much more contemporary. This is a wonderful example of playing with a historical style and liberating it from its own past, doing something so odd to it that it is not just a simple memory of the style. You can't call this version of that vernacular mere appropriation, this manipulation becomes something quite original and interesting.

25

Brochure ブローシュア

Avset Brochure Finland 1993

AD,D:Ilkka Kärkkäiren DF:Dynamo

CL:Avset

Mellor Roman

ABCDEFGHIJKLMNOPQRSTUVWXYZ
abcdefghijklmnopqrstuvwxyz
1234567890$¢&()[]&?!½¼¾—"""«»*'`·····
ßŒøfifflß¼¼AÁÀÄEÉÈÊÒ...½¾¼¼%½½½¾¾

Excellence in typography is the result of nothing more than an attitude. Its appeal comes from the understanding used in its planning; the designer must care. In contemporary advertising the perfect integration of design elements often demands unorthodox typography. It may require the use of compact spacing, minus leading, unusual sizes and weights; whatever is needed to improve appearance and impact. Stating specific principles or goals on the subject of typography is difficult because the principles...

Pipa, in the plucked string group, the leading instrument is the pipa. It is a pear-shaped, lute-like instrument with four strings. The pipa makes a good solo or ensemble instrument. Its ancestor could well be the Persian barbat, but because the Chinese have used it for so many years and have developed so many different techniques for playing it, the pipa is considered to be characteristic of Chinese music.

Present

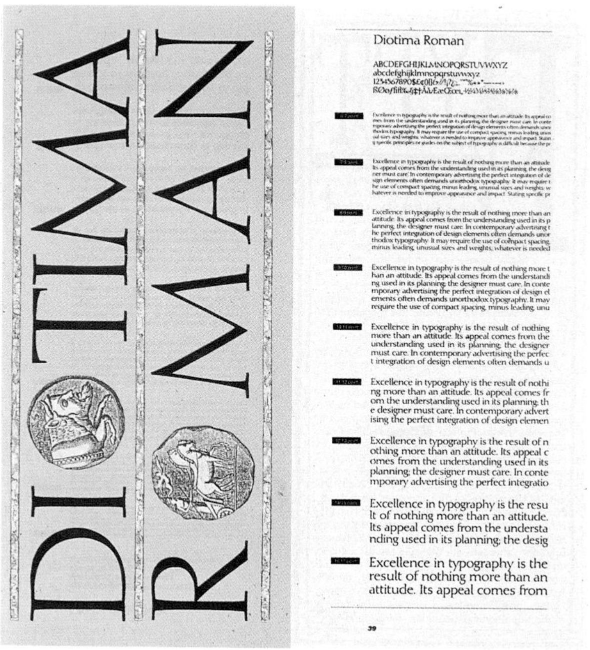

ABCDEFGHIJKLMNOPQRSTUVWXYZ
abcdefghijklmnopqrstuvwxyz
1234567890$¢&()[]&?!½¼¾—"""«»*'`·····
ßŒøfifflß¼¼AÁÀÄEÉÈÊÒ...½¾¼¼%½½½¾¾

Excellence in typography is the result of nothing more than an attitude. Its appeal comes from the understanding used in its planning; the designer must care. In contemporary advertising the perfect integration of design elements often demands unorthodox typography...

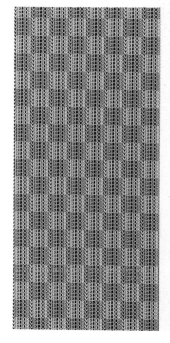

Diotima Roman

ABCDEFGHIJKLMNOPQRSTUVWXYZ
abcdefghijklmnopqrstuvwxyz
1234567890$¢&()[]&?!½¼¾—"""«»*'`·····
ßŒøfifflß¼¼AÁÀÄEÉÈÊÒ...½¾¼¼%½½½¾¾

Excellence in typography is the result of nothing more than an attitude. Its appeal comes from the understanding used in its planning; the designer must care. In contemporary advertising the perfect integration of design elements often demands unorthodox typography. It may require the use of compact spacing, minus leading, unusual sizes and weights; whatever is needed to improve appearance and impact. Stating specific principles or goals on the subject of typography is difficult because the principles...

ESTHETICS

Gilbert Keith Chesterton 1874-1936

Eras Light

ABCDEFGHIJKLMNOPQRSTUVWXYZ
abcdefghijklmnopqrstuvwxyz
1234567890$¢&()[]&?!½¼¾—"""«»*'`·····
ßŒøfifflß¼¼AÁÀÄEÉÈÊÒ...½¾¼¼%½½½¾¾

Excellence in typography is the result of nothing more than an attitude. Its appeal comes from the understanding used in its planning; the designer must care. In contemporary advertising the perfect integration of design elements often demands unorthodox typography...

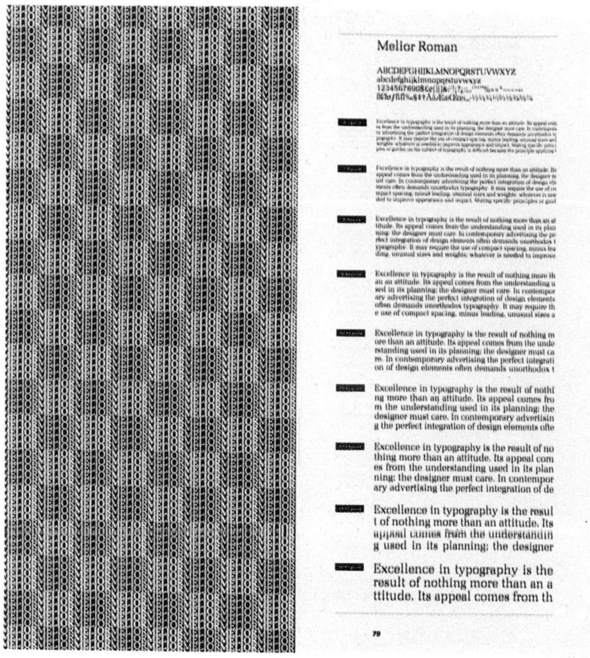

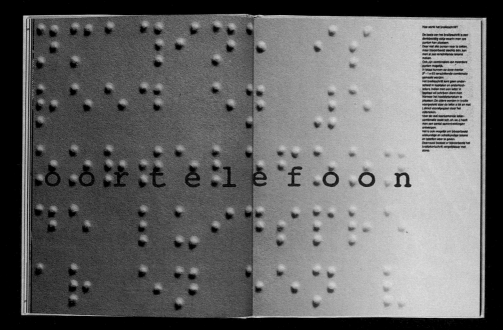

B o o k 本

X'mas Issue The Netherlands 1988

CD:Joost Klinkenberg CD,D:Wim Verboven D:Frans Lieshout P:Sherry Kamp

DF:Total Design CL:KVGO (Koninklijk Verbond voor Grafische Ondernemingen)

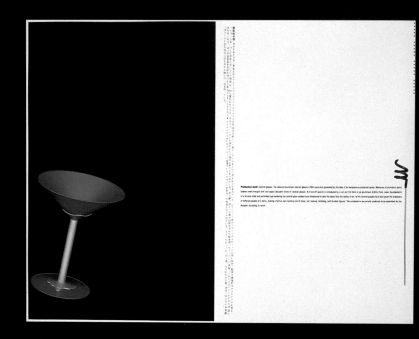

Magazine Spreads 雑誌ページ
Dan Takasugi "Club Irregulars" Nos.7, 12 Japan 1992
CD:Noriko Tetsuka AD,D:Heiquiti Harata
DF:heiquiti harata, EDiX and associates CL:Seirindo & zeit

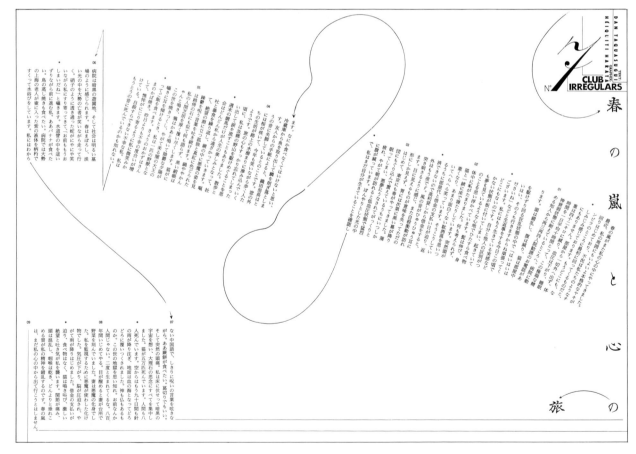

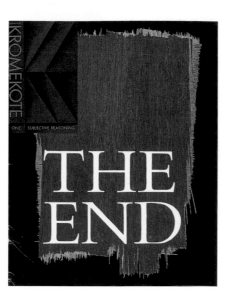

Brochure ブローシュア

Subjective Reasoning "The End" USA 1992

D：Stephen Doyle

DF：Drenttel Doyle Partners CL：Champion International

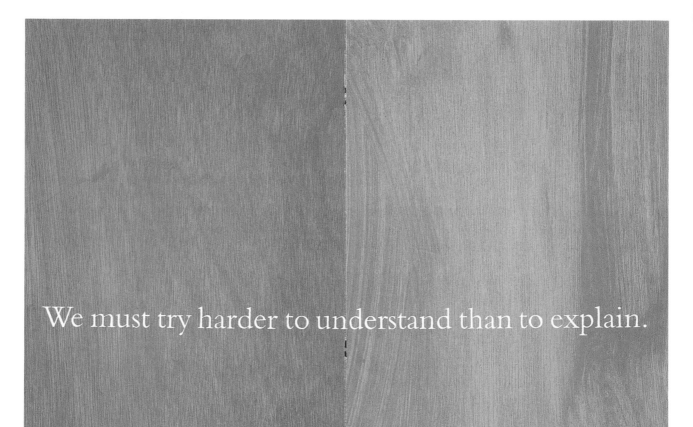

We must try harder to understand than to explain.

MINISTRY OF EDUCATION

WITHIN THE COUNCIL OF STATE (GOVERNMENT) EDUCATIONAL AND CULTURAL ADMINISTRATION COMES UNDER THE MINISTRY OF EDUCATION. THE MINISTRY'S WORK CAN BE SAID TO RELATE TO THE WHOLE LIFESPAN OF AN INDIVIDUAL AND INCLUDES THE FOLLOWING: BASIC GENERAL EDUCATION, VOCATIONAL TRAINING, HIGHER AND ADULT EDUCATION; SCIENCE AND RESEARCH; THE ARTS; YOUTH AFFAIRS; SPORTS; FINANCIAL SUPPORT OF STUDENTS; COPYRIGHT; AND ECCLESIASTICAL AFFAIRS. FINLAND'S PARTICIPATION IN INTERNATIONAL EDUCATIONAL, CULTURAL AND SCIENTIFIC COOPERATION IS ALSO ADMINISTERED BY THE MINISTRY OF EDUCATION. THE ANNUAL STATE BUDGET ILLUSTRATES WELL THE EXTENT AND RELATIVE IMPORTANCE OF THE EDUCATIONAL AND CULTURAL ADMINISTRATION. THE APPROPRIATION OF THE MINISTRY OF EDUCATION IS THE SECOND LARGEST IN THE WHOLE GOVERNMENT. IN RECENT YEARS THE EDUCATIONAL AND CULTURAL BUDGET HAS TOTALLED 25 MILLIARD MARKS, WHICH IS ABOUT 17% OF THE WHOLE ANNUAL STATE BUDGET.

THE MINISTRY OF EDUCATION HAS TACKLED SEVERAL MAJOR CHALLENGES IN RECENT YEARS, SUCH AS THE REFORMS OF BASIC GENERAL, UPPER SECONDARY AND HIGHER EDUCATION. IMPORTANT FUTURE TASKS ARISING FROM THE CHALLENGES OF THE 1990'S WILL CONSIST OF THE DEVELOPMENT OF VOCATIONAL ADULT EDUCATION AND ART EDUCATION.

THE PRESENT TECHNOLOGICAL PROGRESS AND THE SUBSEQUENT SOCIAL CHANGES ARE REFLECTED IN A NUMBER OF NEW ISSUES FACING THE MINISTRY AT PRESENT, SUCH AS A GROWING NEED FOR INSTRUCTION RELATED TO INFORMATION TECHNOLOGY AND ITS DEVELOPMENT. THE DEVELOPING MEDIA CULTURE ALSO MAKES NEW KIND OF CHALLENGING BUT INTERESTING DEMANDS ON THE MINISTRY.

WITH AN INCREASING AMOUNT OF FREE TIME AT THEIR DISPOSAL, CITIZENS EXPECT EVER MORE FROM CULTURAL PROVISION. THE BEST WAY TO RESPOND TO STRUCTURAL CHANGES IS THROUGH EDUCATION. THE EDUCATIONAL AND CULTURAL FIELDS WILL ALSO CREATE AN INCREASING NUMBER OF JOBS IN THE FUTURE.

Brochure Spread ブローシュアページ
Ministry of Education Finland 1990
AD,D:Harri Heikkilä I:Ilkka kärkkäinen
DF:Harri Heikkilä CL:Finland Minstry of Education

Brochure Spread ブローシュアページ
Passport USA 1993
AD:Mark Oldach D:Don Emery
DF:Mark Oldach Design CL:Closer Look Entertainment

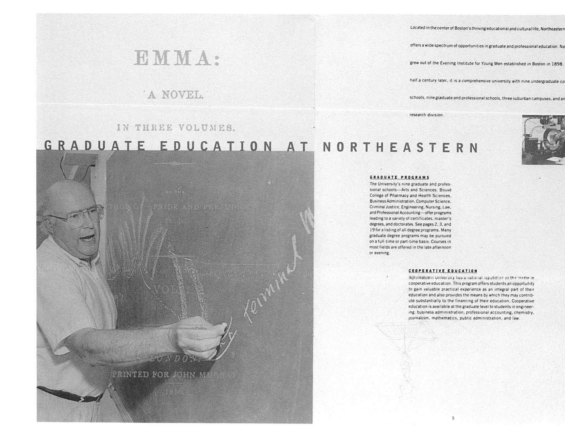

Brochure Spread ブローシュアページ

Graduate School of The Arts and Sciences USA 1992

CD.AD:Clifford Stoltze D::Bob Beerman

DF:Clifford Stoltze Design CL:Northeastern University

EMMA:

A NOVEL.

IN THREE VOLUMES.

GRADUATE EDUCATION AT NORTHEASTERN

Located in the center of Boston's thriving educational and cultural life, Northeastern University offers a wide spectrum of opportunities in graduate and professional education. Northeastern grew out of the Evening Institute for Young Men established in Boston in 1898. More than half a century later, it is a comprehensive university with nine undergraduate colleges and schools, nine graduate and professional schools, three suburban campuses, and an extensive research division.

GRADUATE PROGRAMS

The University's nine graduate and professional schools—Arts and Sciences, Bouvé College of Pharmacy and Health Sciences, Business Administration, Computer Science, Criminal Justice, Engineering, Nursing, Law, and Professional Accounting—offer programs leading to a variety of certificates, master's degrees, and doctorates. See pages 2, 3, and 19 for a listing of all degree programs. Many graduate degree programs may be pursued on a full-time or part-time basis. Courses in most fields are offered in the late afternoon or evening.

COOPERATIVE EDUCATION

Northeastern University has a national reputation as the leader in cooperative education. This program offers students an opportunity to gain valuable practical experience as an integral part of their education and also provides the means by which they may contribute substantially to the financing of their education. Cooperative education is available at the graduate level to students in engineering, business administration, professional accounting, chemistry, journalism, mathematics, public administration, and law.

Brochure Spread ブローシュアページ

MarketPlace Business USA 1992

AD.D:Anita Meyer, Karin Fickett D:Matthew Monk P:Tony Rinaldo

CW:Catherine Engelke DF:plus design CL:MarketPlace Information

You can export any MarketPlace list or report to other software packages—Macintosh or IBM-compatible. So if you've got your existing leads in a tracking package on your PC, or if you want to use the mail-merge program on your Macintosh, there's no need for you to change your way of working.

Export to other software packages

Most list sources require you to pay extra to use a list more than once. Not so with MarketPlace. Once you finalize a MarketPlace list, you are free to use that list as often as you like for an entire year.

Use your list repeatedly

You can sort MarketPlace lists in any number of ways. If you want mailing labels in ZIP+4 order, but prospect records in alphabetical order, MarketPlace can handle it.

Sort your list

③ USE YOUR LIST

in the form that's most convenient for you

Not sure that your mailing piece is effective? MarketPlace lets you create random samples of your lists, making it easy to fit lists into your budget and to create small test lists.

Create a random sample

Merge your list with other MarketPlace lists

MarketPlace offers you a number of options for combining records from two MarketPlace lists, including the ability to locate and remove duplicate records.

Choose from a wide variety of output options

You get over 40 mailing-label formats (covering the complete line of Avery labels). MarketPlace also gives you the option of title-addressing, and prints your labels in upper- and lowercase for professional-looking direct mail. You can also use predefined and custom report formats for creating call sheets, telemarketing reports, and prospect lists.

Annual Report アニュアル・リポート
Lasertechnics USA 1992
AD,D:Steve Wedeen P:Michael Barley CW:Lasertechnics
DF:Vaughn/Wedeen Creative CL:Lasertechnics

Understanding limits and REDEFINING boundaries

MOVING FORWARD

Not too long ago, we would have described ourselves as being in the field of architecture and interior design. Today we realize that we are actually in the business of solving our clients' facilities problems through value-added design services. The two may not appear to be very different, but the distinction opens up extraordinary opportunities and immensely expands our horizons. We anticipate that by the turn of the century our firm's services will have assumed even greater scope and diversity.

A business revolution is currently in progress across the globe. This revolution involves people who are seeking more control of their lives, more value to the things that they do, and more personal freedoms. The revolution is spawning change, and the pace of change is accelerating, particularly as work habits shift, life-styles evolve and baby-boomers step into middle age.

We believe the best way to leverage change is to anticipate it, and our management team has therefore identified long-term opportunities for our future growth. Our mandate is to redefine our business and to expand globally. This has resulted in our expanding into Europe and Asia, strengthening our position in diversified fields such as transportation, strategic planning and master planning, biotechnology, and government-related projects, and in reaching out to new business opportunities, such as product and technology-enhanced design.

[3

Annual Report アニュアル・リポート
Architects 1992 USA 1992
AD:John Bricker D:Mary Tesluk
DF:Gensler and Associates/Graphics CL:Gensler and Associates/Architects

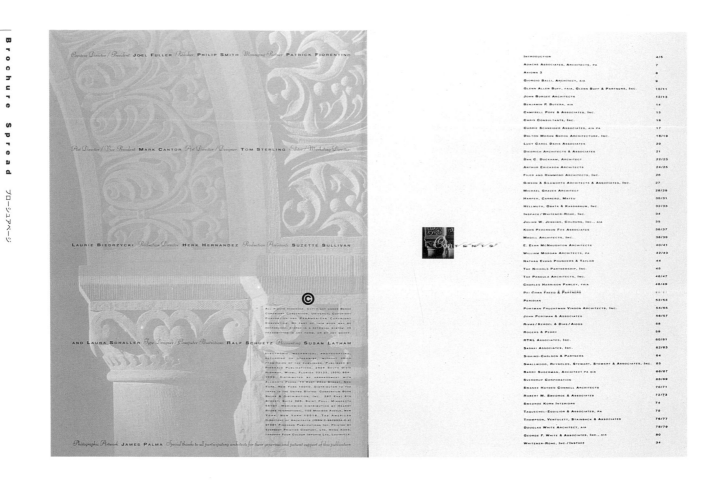

Brochure Spread ブローシュアページ
The American Directory of Architects USA 1990
CD,AD:Joel Fuller AD,D:Tom Sterling
P:James Palma DF:Pinkhaus Design CL:Pinkhaus Publication

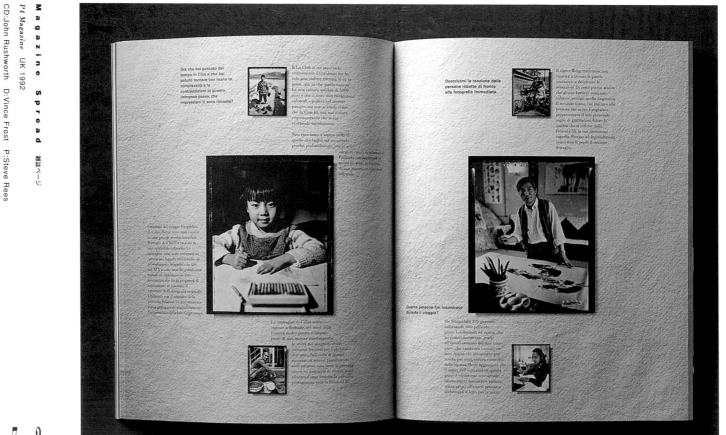

Magazine Spread 雑誌ページ
P4 Magazine UK 1992
CD:John Rushworth D:Vince Frost P:Steve Rees
DF:Pentagram Design CL:Polaroid

Christmas Card クリスマス・カード

Family USA 1991
AD:Mark Oldach D:Don Emery, Laura Gammerelli
CW:Linda Chryle DF:Mark Oldach Design CL:Mark Oldach Design

It is
the child
of the
child

who
has come to see
what it means
to be part
of the
family.

There are no straight paths, only circles of understanding where friends become family, family become friends.

Wishing my child
to know the family
i came to know.

Holding fingers,
walking boldly with "boppa".
Gentle "nanny"
tugging at my imagination
with fairy tales and fables.
Teasing cousins, sassy aunts and winking uncles
challenging
me with twice-told tales of family adventures.

DO I UNDERSTAND THE LIFE-LONG WISDOM

THAT ANSWERED MY CHILD-LIKE WONDER?

what's   in   a   face

and

what's   beneath   those   eyes

is this for real

or

is it merely a disguise

deeper
than
skin

is the

beauty

eye   admire

deeper than skin

is the love i desire

Brochure Spread ブローシュアページ

DIFFA Invitation   USA 1991

AD,D:Jeff Fabian, Jean Kane, Sam Shelton   P:Geof Kern   CW:Cheryl Duvall

CL:Design Industries Foundation for AIDS: DC Chapter   CL:Beechwood Music   CL:Beechwood Music   CL:Beechwood Music

gilbert oxford

Brochure ブローシュア
Gilbert Oxford   USA 1992
CD,AD,D:Joel Fuller   AD,D:Claudia Decastro
P:Gallen Mei   DF Pinkhaus Design   CL:Su McGlouchlin/Gilbert Paper

IT IS
SAID THAT
THE ONLY
CONSTANT
IS CHANGE.

Yet the French have an expression, "Plus ca change, plus c'est la meme chose". (The more things change, the more they stay the same.) Do things really change or not? Perhaps it's a matter of degree. Maybe small things are always changing, while the important things remain constant. So fashion is a fleeting thing, **while style transcends time.** Or, as the song goes: "A kiss is still a kiss, page 24 →

a sigh
IS STILL A SIGH,
THE FUNDAMENTAL
THINGS APPLY
AS TIME GOES BY."

The fundamental things apply. The feel of silk on skin. The Force of simple, honest words. The texture of a fine paper stock. The sculpted lines of a classic car. Why do certain things become classics? Is it a perfect marriage of page 54 →

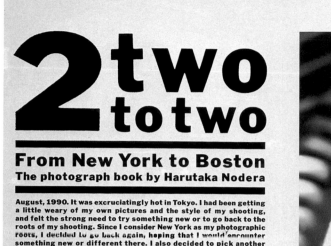

2 two to two

From New York to Boston
The photograph book by Harutaka Nodera

August, 1990. It was excruciatingly hot in Tokyo. I had been getting a little weary of my own pictures and the style of my shooting, and felt the strong need to try something new or to go back to the roots of my shooting. Since I consider New York as my photographic roots, I decided to go back again, hoping that I would encounter something new or different there. I also decided to pick another city, Boston, to visit, only because it was close enough from New York and was full of old streets and buildings. Of course, I could try some of their famous lobsters while visiting there. To me, New York is jazz and coffee, while Boston stands for classical music and tea. It's that simple. I took an airshuttle from New York to Boston. It was just like taking a bus ride. Fifty minutes in the air. The two cities showed me such a variety of different faces in 24 hours. Having remembered the same taste of the mustard on a $1 hotdog, I found myself again thoroughly enjoying taking pictures.

Book Spread ブックページ　Japan 1992
"Two to Two" Harutaka Nodera Photo Book
AD,D:Yoichirou Fujii　D:Hiroyuki Suzuki　P:Harutaka Nodera
DF:Bakery 37.1　CL:Slow Hand

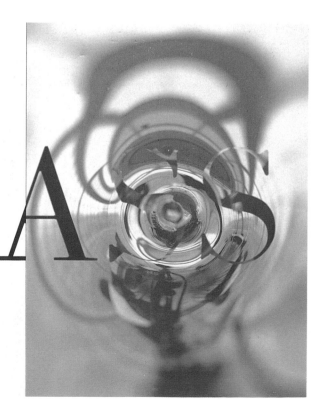

GLASS

ガラスの長い歴史の中でも、透明な板ガラスをつくるために、
さまざまな手法が試みられ、また現在に至るまでに長いときを要したのです。
まずヨーロッパでは、手吹きの円筒ガラスを切り開く方法が発達し、20世紀初めまでは、
これが最もなめらかな表面、つまり透明度の高いガラスを得る方法でした。
鉄の型に流し込む方法は、表面に型の跡が残り、磨き工程が必要だったからです。
製造工程で、空気が入ったり歪みを生じたものは、いわば失敗作であり、
壊して作り直されたり、庶民の行くパブなどで使われました。ところが、
透明で平らな板ガラスが容易に得られる現代に於いては、そうした歪みなどの
味わいが逆に評価され、意図的に作られるようになったのが、面白いところでしょう。
1階のラウンジに使われた、ヘソのあるガラスは、そんな歴史を語ってくれます。
一方、ヨーロッパの宗教建築などを彩った、ステンドグラス。ここ帝都ホテルでは
使われています。色ガラスの中でも、金や銅を用いて発色させる深紅は、
最も出しにくい高価な色。16世紀のイギリスに残る紋章をデザインにとり、
当時の製法で作られたその色合いを、ぜひ御覧いただきたいものの1つです。

Brochure Spreads ブローシュアページ
Hotel Book　Japan 1992
CD:Satoru Miyata　AD:Hiroaki Nagai　D:Kyoko Iida　P:Kiyomi Tagawa
CW:Yuri Hirano　Producer:Taeko Negishi　DF:N.G.　CL:Shinnichi Trading

Brochure Spreads ブローシュアページ
Hotel Book Japan 1992
CD:Satoru Miyata AD:Hiroaki Nagai D:Kyoko Iida P:Kiyomi Tagawa
CW:Yuri Hirano Producer:Taeko Negishi DF:N.G. CL:Shinnichi Trading

Brochure ブローシュア
"*Moderns*" Japan 1992
CD:Masato Handa Assistant Director: Kenji Takazawa
D:Hiroshi Ichimaru DF:Out Side Directors CL:Banyu
AD.D:Osamu Sato

MODERNS 2

Banyu Pharmaceutical Co.,Ltd.
これが萬有製薬のもう一つの顔だ。
とても日本的な社名でありながら、萬有製薬は外資系企業だ。
製薬における世界のリーディングカンパニー、
米国メルク社の"メルクグループ"の一員である。

Banyu Pharmaceutical Co.,Ltd.

世界で最も高いレベルの研究開発力を誇る医薬品メーカーが、米国メルク社だ。
メルク社は"研究のメルク"と呼ばれるほど、研究開発に力を注いでいる。
毎年売上高の10%以上を研究開発費に投入し、その額は約10億ドル。
世界7カ国に17の研究所。
生産は世界18カ国47の工場で行なわれている。
またメルク社は単に医薬品業界のトップであるというだけではない。
米国のフォーチュン誌が毎年発表する
"America's Most Admired Corporations (アメリカの最も賞賛される企業)
ランキングで6年連続第1位に選ばれている。

萬有製薬とメルク社の関係は、1952年にはじまった。メルク社の製品を、萬有製薬が輸入販売したことがきっかけだ。2年後、合弁会社"日本メルク萬有"を設立。メルク社の開発した医家向け医薬品を、日本メルク萬有が製造し、萬有製薬が販売するというスタイルで信頼関係を築いてきた。そしてこの協力体制と信頼は、1984年に萬有製薬がメルクグループの一員となることで一層強化された。米国企業が日本企業に資本参加した場合、またその逆でも、すべてがうまくいくとは限らない。萬有製薬とメルク社は、長年の信頼関係、お互いに良く似た社風、自主

性と独立性の尊重などによって、最も成功している事例と評価されている。
またメルク社は1991年、世界最大の総合化学メーカーとして名高いデュポン社との合弁で、デュポンメルク社を設立した。2つの親会社がともに業界を代表する巨大企業だけに、その将来は大いに注目されている。萬有製薬はこのデュポンメルク社と今後日本市場において広範な協力関係に入ることで合意している。将来、萬有製薬から独創的な新薬が登場することは間違いない。

4   5

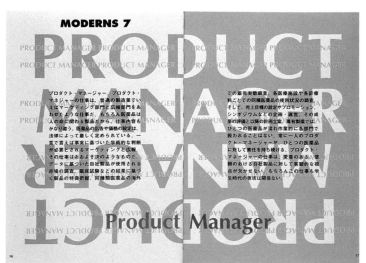

MODERNS 7

プロダクト・マネージャー、プロダクト・マネジャーの仕事は、普通の製造業でいえばマーケティング部門と広報部門あわせたような仕事だ。もちろん医薬品は人の命に関わる製品だから、仕事内容もかなり違う。医薬品の広告や価格の設定は、法律によって厳しく定められている。一言で言えば事実に基づいた学術的な判断が必要とされるマーケティングと広報。その仕事はおおよそ次のようなものだ。データに基づいた自社製品が使用される市場の調査。臨床試験などの結果に基づく製品の特徴把握。同種類医薬品の海外

での販売実態調査。各医療施設や各診療科ごとの同種医薬品の使用状況の調査。そして、売上目標の設定やプロモーション、シンポジウムなどの企画・運営。その成果の評価と以降の計画立案。萬有製薬では、ひとつの医薬品が流れ作業的に各部門で扱われることはない。常に一人のプロダクト・マネージャーが、ひとつの医薬品に対して責任を持ち続ける。プロダクト・マネージャーの仕事は、愛着のある、信頼のおける自社製品に対して客観的な視点が欠かせない。もちろんこの仕事も学生時代の専攻は関係ない。

Product Manager

16   17

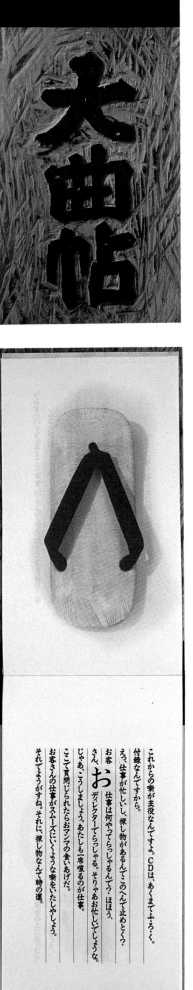

Booklet ブックレット
Daikyokucho Japan 1991
AD,D,P,I:Yoichiro, Fujii D:Sayoko Ueno, Keiko Maekawa
DF:Bakery 37.1 CL:CS Artist

それでようがすね。それに、探し物なんて時の運。
お客さんの仕事がスムーズにいくような新を、いたしやしょう。
ここで買閉じられたらおマンマの食い、あげだ。
じゃあ、こうしましょう。あたしも一席喋るのが仕事。
さん、ディレクターでらっしゃる。そりゃあお忙しいでしょうな、
お客、**お**仕事は何やってらっしゃるんで？ほほう、
えっ、仕事が忙しいし、探し物があるんでこの人で止めとく？
付録なんてすから。
これからの新が主役なんですよ。CDは、あくまでふろ一く。

Brochure Spreads ブローシュアスページ

2nd Impression Newsletter USA 1991

AD:Mark Oldach DF:Mark Oldach Design

CL:First Impression Printers and Lithgraphers

At First Impression, we're not interested in issuing HALF-hearted statements or speaking in DOUBLE-talk. We're not promoting SECOND hand ideas, SECOND rate solutions, or SECOND string support. But we will confess to being BI-partisan, convinced that there *are* TWO ways about it. With this, the SECOND coming of "Impression," we want you to understand that there is an affordable, simple way to attain TWICE the power for *effective* communications. You *can* have it BOTH ways if you stop thinking of TWO-color printing as SECOND rate. You won't be im-PAIRED when you realize how TWO-color printing can be the DOUBLE-edged solution that provides un-equivocal practicality and inventiveness. You can

Vietnamese: **HAI**
Spanish **DOS**
French **DEUX**
Hawaiian **LUA**
Italian **DUE**
Rumanian **DOUI**
Latin **DUO**
or **BINI**

CAN WE HAVE YOUR UNDIVIDED ATTENTION PLEASE?

Gaelic **DHA**
Croatian **DVA**
Polish **DWA**
Japanese **NI, FUTATSU**
Norwegian **TO**
Swedish **TVÅ**
Dutch **TWEE**
German **ZWEI**

achieve infinite *creativity* and produce *economical* communications with a mere TWO colors. There is nothing BI-partisan about our BI-ased point of view. BI-form printing need not BI-furcate the effect you want to achieve (*figure that one out!*). You'll be dancing the TWO-step when you re-DEUCE your constraints, re-DOUBLE your efforts and COUPLE your *imagination* with TWO-color printing that is SECOND to none. How did we come to this TWO-dimensional view? By understanding the *power* of TWOS in all areas of our lives. TWOS are synonomous with unheralded accomplishments throughout human history. Therefore, we dedicate our "2ND Impression" to the *power* of TWOS, particularly those in printing.

Half/
Half

DOUBLE TALK

Somebody has been double dealing when it comes to double entendres. These words or phrases are supposed to have two meanings. But alas! We've been double crossed—duped even—by a slew of double entendres that are two-faced because they represent a contradiction in "two" terms. After all, how can there be a "duet for one"? Why does a "two-step" entail three steps? And why does a "pair royal" in cribbage and other card games mean three-of-a-kind? Who is the culprit behind these confusing paradoxes? Stay "two-ned" for more information.

Second choice doesn't have to mean second rate. If you want to create crisper, deeper halftones, consider using duotones. Duotones are two-color reproductions from a one color photograph. By using a deep gray or blue, you can intensify the contrasts between the light and dark areas of your halftone. Duotones can be produced with any color; you can communicate a special mood or effect by using an unusual or bright second color. So think twice about these halftones!

DOUBLE VISION

An eye for an eye for an eye and you're seeing double. *Diplopia* is the technical term for double vision, which is the perception of two images from a single object. It is most commonly caused by temporary or permanent paralysis of the eye muscle and is one of the first signs of botulism and myasthenia gravis (to say nothing of drinking too much).

However, it's important not to confuse diplopia with other twos of the eyes. For example, you can't use bifocals to correct double vision. Bifocals are eyeglasses with lenses that are split into two. Half the lenses correct for nearsightedness and half correct for farsightedness. Benjamin Franklin was the first to experiment with designing bifocal lenses so that he could glance up from reading and enjoy scenery on trips. But bifocals didn't become popular until the 1820s, when enough people had access to regular glasses that they tired of having to change from reading to distance lenses.

And don't start thinking that if the eye doctor checks your vision twice you've had a double refraction, unless you're Shirley MacLaine. Double refraction is really an optical property of crystals. Also known as birefringence, double refraction occurs when a single ray of light entering a crystal is split into two rays, each travelling in a different direction. One ray, called the extraordinary ray, becomes bent, or refracted. Calcites, ice, mica, quartz, sugar and tourmaline are all examples of crystals that will double refract. Who knows—maybe by playing with double refracting crystals you'll discover a supernatural property that will give you second sight.

TWO WRONGS DO NOT MAKE A RIGHT.

JOEL FULLER

CHAIRMAN'S STATEMENT

just
the beginning

Brochure Spread ブローシュアページ

1992 Biannual Show USA 1992

CD,AD.:Joel Fuller AD,D:Mark Cantor P.:Jose Molina

DF:Pinkhaus Design CL:AIGA, Miami Chapter

Brochure Spread ブローシュアページ

Paper Australia 1992

D.I:David Lancashire DF:David Lancashire Design

CL:Dalton Fine Paper

Book 本
"*Arata Isozaki Works 30*" Japan 1992
AD:Kaoru Kasai D:Hiroshi Kichise
DF:Sun-Ad CL:Rikuyo-sha Publishing

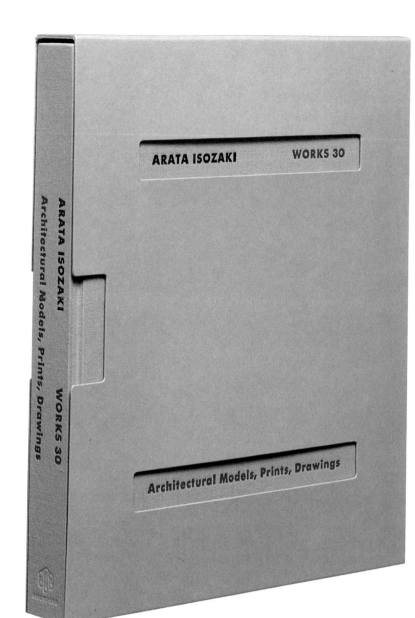

In the beginning was an ending.
For example, the ending which was the year 1968. Arata Isozaki compares this year to 1527, the year of "the plunder of Rome (il sacco di Roma)." Just as the emptiness which emerged from the loss of Rome as center gave birth to a mannerism filled with irony, so after the progressive movement of modernism came to a dead end, the architect had no choice but to indulge in an ironical game of signs, alluding to the various styles of ancient and modern times, of East and West. It is a fact that the representative works of Arata Isozaki, including the Tsukuba Center Building, were built "after the end of modernism," in the season whose names, for that reason, include "the post-modern"; in that sense it is no mistake to see this architect as a representative post-modernist.
The architect as this sort of post-modernist appears as a sophisticated ironist. He hasn't the slightest belief in any of the various styles—especially his own original ones. For him they are dead in advance, or they have ended in advance. And yet, for that very reason he does not feel the need to directly renounce them, if anything, he flatters them gazing at them from behind the glass with the cold enthusiasm of a dissector and, by a skillful manipulation of the magic hand, can even come up with a collage which might, to borrow an expression from the Surrealists, be called "un cadavre exquis." It is the ironist's strategy to thus stand on an absolutely safe high ground by anticipating the ending, and to maintain a higher-dimensional subjectivity by denying

his own subjectivity.
In fact it is possible, and even perhaps inevitable, to see examples of such irony here and there in Arata Isozaki's architecture. They appear, not like the architect's affirmative answer to a problem, but rather like a puzzle that has anticipated its solution in advance. The Tsukuba Center Building is a good example. Each of the elements alluded to here with an astonishingly intricate manner, and combined to produce a deliberately discordant sound, is clearly narrated—"This is Michelangelo," "This is Ledoux," and it is even revealed that such historical sources and the mutual relations among them do not possess any necessary meaning at all. Furthermore, as the critic is about to point that out, the architect himself, a prolific writer of great eloquence, has already gone way beyond him by virtue of his extensive self-interpretation. Thus the architect, a most talkative Sphinx , always wins, and the viewer stands helpless before the perfectly seamless exterior, dazzled by the cold glaze, full of sterile sensuality, of aluminum panels and glass blocks.
However, is this really everything? Here we must remember: didn't Arata Isozaki, in the year 1968, considered "the end of modernism," present, at the Milano Triennale, another "ending," a vision of the future city in ruins superimposed on an image of the devastation of Hiroshima immediately after the atomic bomb was dropped? In fact this post-modernist has been active since long before 1968 and, while he did describe a vision of the immense future city which in one

初めに終わりがあった。
たとえば1968年という終わり、磯崎新はこの年を1527年を「ローマ掠奪」の年になぞらえている。ローマという中心の喪失からくる空虚感が、アイロニーに満ちたマニエリスムを生んだように、モダニズムの前進運動が行き詰まりに入ったあと、建築家は古今東西の様々な様式を全面的にアイロニカルな延引する記号のゲームに取るしかなくなる。そうした「モダニズムの終わりの後」——その季節でのポストモダンと呼ばれもした季節に、つくばセンタービルをはじめとする磯崎新の代表作も作られていったのは事実だし、その点でおおいにこの建築家を代表的なポストモダンと見なすことも間違っているわけではない。

そのようなポストモダンとしての建築家は、洗練されたアイロニストとして現われるだろう。彼は、様々なる様式——とりわけ自らのオリジナルなそれ——をいささかも信じていない、彼によって、それらはあらかじめ死んだ、あるいは終わったものなのだ。しかし、だからこそ、彼はそれらを真向から否定する必要もない。それどころか、彼はガラスの向こうから解剖学者の冷たい熱狂を帯びて見据えてそれらを審め尽くし、マジック・ハンドを巧みに操って——シュールレアリストの表現を借りれば——「精妙なる死体」とも言うべきコラージュを作りあげさえすることさえできるのである。こうして、終わりを先取りすることによって絶対安全な高所に立ち、自己の主体を否定してみせる

ことによって高次の主体性を維持するというのが、アイロニストの戦略である。
実際、磯崎新の建築のそこここにそういったアイロニーを見て取れることは十分だし可能かつできるほどだろう。それらは、与えられた課題に対する建築家の前向きな解答というより、謎——それもあらかじめ先取りしたイメージのように見える。つくばセンタービルがよい例だ。驚くほど巧妙な手法でそこに引用され、意図的な不協和音を奏でるように組み込まれた建築の一つひとつとは、これはミケランジェロだ、ルドゥだ、とあからさまに語られており、しかも、こうした歴史的な出典や相互の間の必然的な意味もないことをさえ白日してしまっている。しかも、批評家がそれを指摘しようと思った時には、雄弁な饒舌家

である建築家自身が厖大な自己注釈によってさんざんと先を越しているというわけだ。こうして、饒舌なスフィンクスとしての建築家はいつも勝利し、見るものは、一分の隙もない表層の輝き、アルミ・パネルやガラス・ブロックの不毛な官能を帯びたために輝き出る冷たい魅力に、なすすべもなく立ちつくす。
しかし、本当にそれですべてなのだろうか。ここで思い出さなければならない「モダニズムの終わり」と位置付けられる1968年に、磯崎新は、ミラノ・トリエンナーレにおいて、もうひとつの「終わり」——原爆投下後の広島の廃墟の惨禍に置かれたような未来都市の廃墟のフィジョンを提示したのではなかったか。実際、このポストモダンは、68年よりはるか以前から活動を続けており、あ

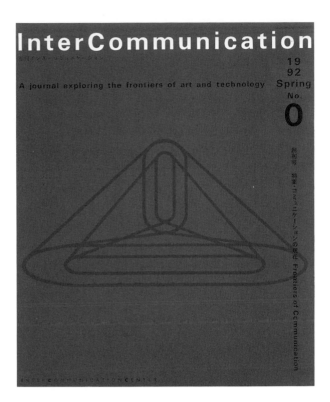

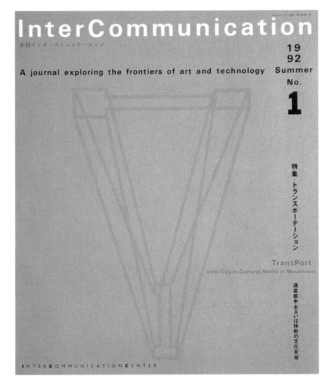

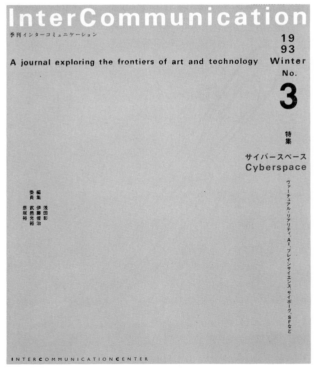

Magazine Covers 雑誌カバー
"Inter Communication" Japan 1992
AD,D:Ichiro Higashiizumi D:Shuichi Miyagishi, Megumi Takeuchi
DF:Huia Media Design CL:NTT Publishing

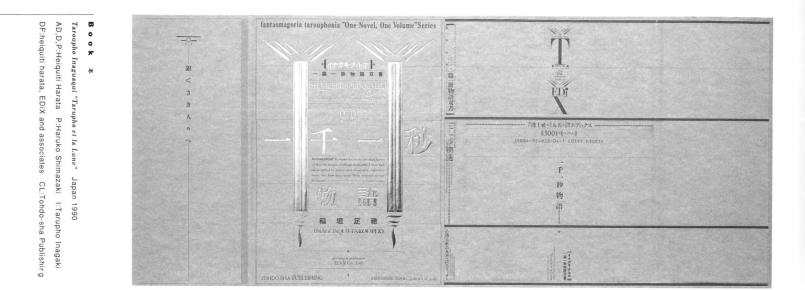

Book 本

Taruopho Inaguaqui "Taruopho et la Lune" Japan 1990
AD,D,P:Heiquiti Harata P:Haruko Shimazaki I:Taruopho Inagaki
DF:heiquiti harata, EDiX and associates CL:Tohdo-sha Publishing

Book 本

"hi-cArat" Japan 1989
CD:Kyoichi Nakagawa AD,D:Heiquiti Harata P:Takayuki Kobayashi
DF:heiquiti harata, EDiX and associates CL:Nijyu-isseikisha

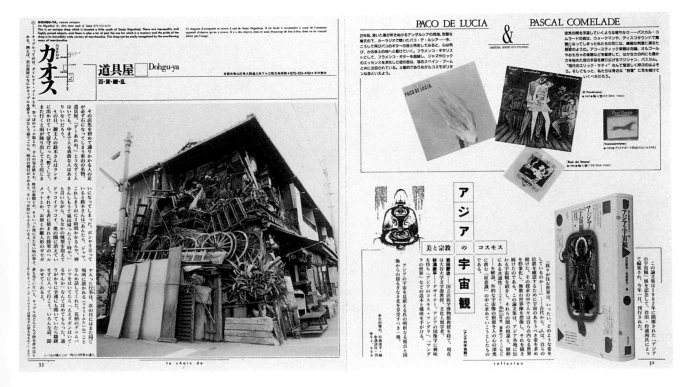

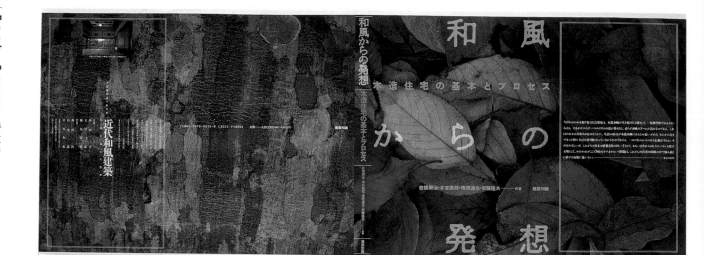

Book Cover ブックカバー

Brainstorming From Japanese Architectural Design Japan 1992

AD,D:Tsuyokatsu Kudo

P:Masao Ota CL:Kenchikuchishiki

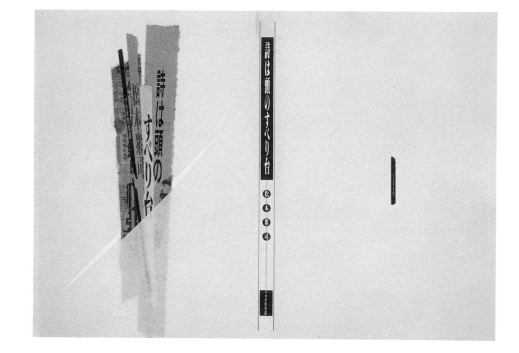

Poetry Book 詩集

"Poem is Sliding Way of head" Japan 1991

AD,D:Yoshimaru Takahashi

CL:Syugi Matsumoto

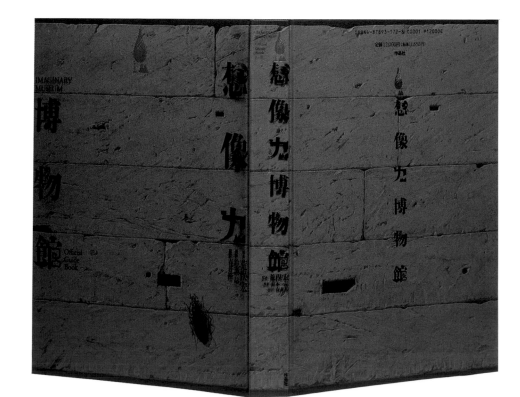

Book Cover ブックカバー

"Imaginary Museum" Japan 1993

D:Hitoshi Suzuki I:Hideki Sugita

CL:Shinjuku-shobo

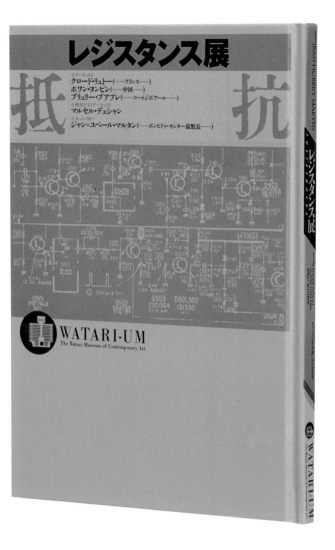

Catalogue カタログ

Résistances Japan 1992

CD:Etsuko Watari AD,D:Heiquiti Harata P:Yoshiharu Watabe, Hiroyuki Mitake

DF:heiquiti harata, EDIX and associates CL:Watari-UM

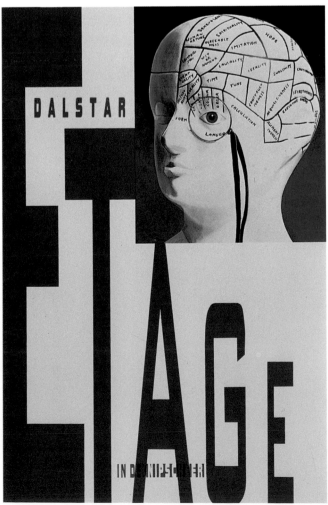

Book Cover ブックカバー

Etage The Netherlands 1992

AD,D:Henrik Barends I:Rob Scholte

DF:Studio Henrik Barends CL:in de Knipscheer Publishers

B o o k 本

"The Museum Inside The Telephone Network" Japan 1992

D:Hitoshi Suzuki, Keiji Terai

CL:NTT (Nippon Telegraph and Telephone)

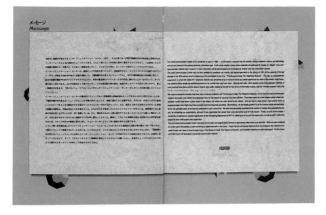

高橋悠治
TAKAHASHI Yuji

もしもし、こちらは城
Hello, I'm Calling from the Castle

INTERACTIVE
Channel
#7102

Access No.
5

▲独自のプログラミングで構築された高橋悠治氏の音楽作品は、
電話回線の向こう側に存在する聴衆との一回限りの対話を実現するもの。
そのシステムは、インタラクティヴな回線制御環境のもとで、
アクセスしたユーザーの時系列上のタイミングを読み取り、
直ちにMacintosh上のプログラムが作曲を開始し、
永遠に演奏を続けるというものである。

▲Yuji Takahashi's musical works, which are constructed with his own special program, create an one-time-only dialogue with the audience at the other end of the phone line. The system is set up to read the timing of the accessing users in diachronic sequence within the interactive controlled environment of the telephone line; the Macintosh program immediately begins composition, and the performance continues indefinitely.

Page
139

System components
●Main CPU
Macintosh SE30
Memory 8MB
Hard Disk 80MB
●Software
MAX
●Sound resource(Sampler)
AKAI S-1100
6MB

Born 1938.
Composer and pianist. Studied under Xenakis,
and was once active in the forefront of Japanese avant-garde music, eg.
using computers in composition,
but in 1978 formed the Water Buffalo Orchestra,
which performed Asian and Latin American protest songs.
Since 1983 Takahashi composes and performs mainly with personal computer and digital samplers.

Catalogue Cover カタログカバー

The Biennale of Venice Japan 1991

AD,D:Kijuro Yahagi

CL:The Japan Foundation

LA BIENNALE DI VENEZIA
QUINTA MOSTRA
INTERNAZIONALE DI
ARCHITETTURA 1991
THE BIENNALE OF VENICE
THE FIFTH INTERNATIONAL
EXHIBITION OF
ARCHITECTURE 1991
ISHII Kazuhiro
ISOZAKI Arata
MAKI Fumihiko
SAKATA Seizo
TAKAMATSU Shin

THE JAPAN FOUNDATION

THE JAPAN FOUNDATION

Calendar Cover カレンダーカバー

FH (Figurative Horizon) Japan 1992

AD,D,P:Kijuro Yahagi

CL:A de S Publishing

FH
Figurative Horizon

Gerrit Thomas Rietveld [1888-1964]

Planning, Photographs, Design and Text by Kijuro Yahagi

ABC|DE|SIGNE
A de S PUBLISHING INC.

Book 本

"Sade, Goya, Mozart" Japan 1991

AD,D:Kijuro Yahagi

CL:Hayakawa Publishing

CD and Book Boxed Set CD,本 ボックスセット

Complete Mozart Edition Japan 1991

AD,D:Kijuro Yahagi

CL:Shogakukan

Book 本

Sinne-Dialektik Ihres Wandels　Japan 1992

AD:Nobuo Nakagaki

D:Tatsuya Ariyama

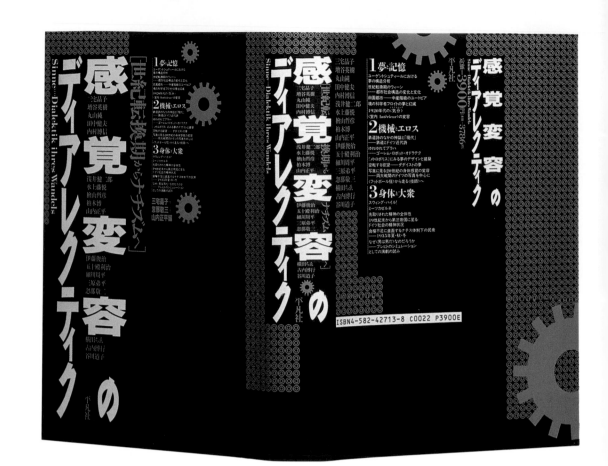

Book 本

"Anthology of A Snake That Is Too Long"　Japan 1989

D:Hitoshi Suzuki　Typesetter:Kiyoaki Inoue

CL:Shinjuku-shobo

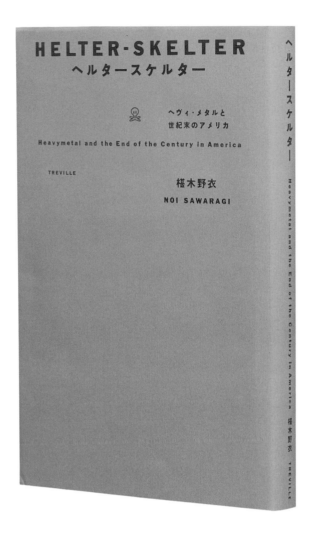

Book 本

"Helter-Skelter" Japan

AD,D:Ichiro Higashiizumi D:Shuichi Miyagishi, Megumi Takeuchi

CW:Kenichi Kawai DF:Huia Media Design CL:Treville

Book 本

"Spontaneous" Japan 1991

AD,D: chiro Higashiizumi

DF:Huia Media Design CL:Shiseido

Book *
"Iroha" Japan 1991
AD.,D:Keita Shinohara
CL:Letterhouse

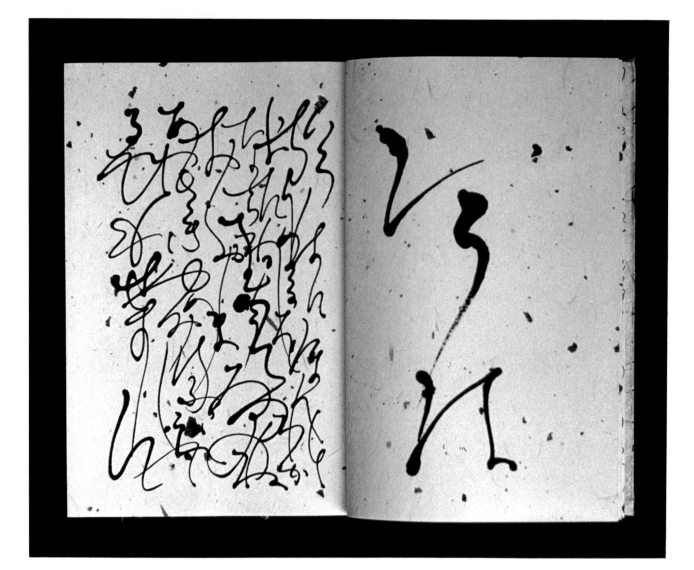

B o o k ✳
Art Directors Club of Europe Volume I (Annual) The Netherlands 1992
CD:Eugene Bay AD,D:Rob Verhaart P:Peter Rauter (Juries) Monique Degenaar (3D work)
I:Leo van Noppen DF:Visser Bay Anders Toscani Design CL:Art Directors Club of Europe

Letterhead Book Cover　レターヘッド・ブックカバー

"Letterhead 100"　Japan 1992

CD:Seiji Koseki　AD,D:Tatsuomi Majima

Artist:Masaharu Takasaki　DF:Majima Design　CL:Gulliver

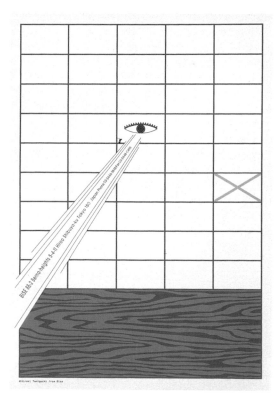

Letterhead Book Pages　レターヘッド・ブックページ

"Letterhead 100"　Japan 1992

CD:Seiji Koseki　AD,D:Tatsuomi Majima　D:Katsuichi Ito,Hiroki Taniguchi

DF:Majima Design　CL:Gulliver

Letterhead Book Pages レターヘッド・ブックページ

"Letterhead 100" Japan 1992
CD:Seiji Koseki AD,D:Tatsuomi Majima D:Shigeo Katsuoka, Noriyuki Tanaka, Yukimasa Okumura,
DF:Majima Design CL:Gulliver

Stationery ステーショナリー

Nakatsuka Daisuke Japan 1992

AD:Daisuke Nakatsuka D:Tadanori Yokoo

DF:Yokoo Tadanori Atelier CL:Nakatsuka Daisuke

Stationery ステーショナリー

Type Gallery USA 1987

AD,D:Rick Eiber DF:Rick Eiber Design (RED)

CL:The Type Gallery

Stationery ステーショナリー

Akiko Hirose   Japan 1988

AD.D:Keisuke Unosawa

DF:Keisuke Unosawa Design   CL:Akiko Hirose

Stationery ステーショナリー

DCM Letterhead   Australia 1990

CD.:Garry Emery   AD.D:Emery Vincent Design

DF:Emery Vincent Design   CL.:Denton Corker Marshall

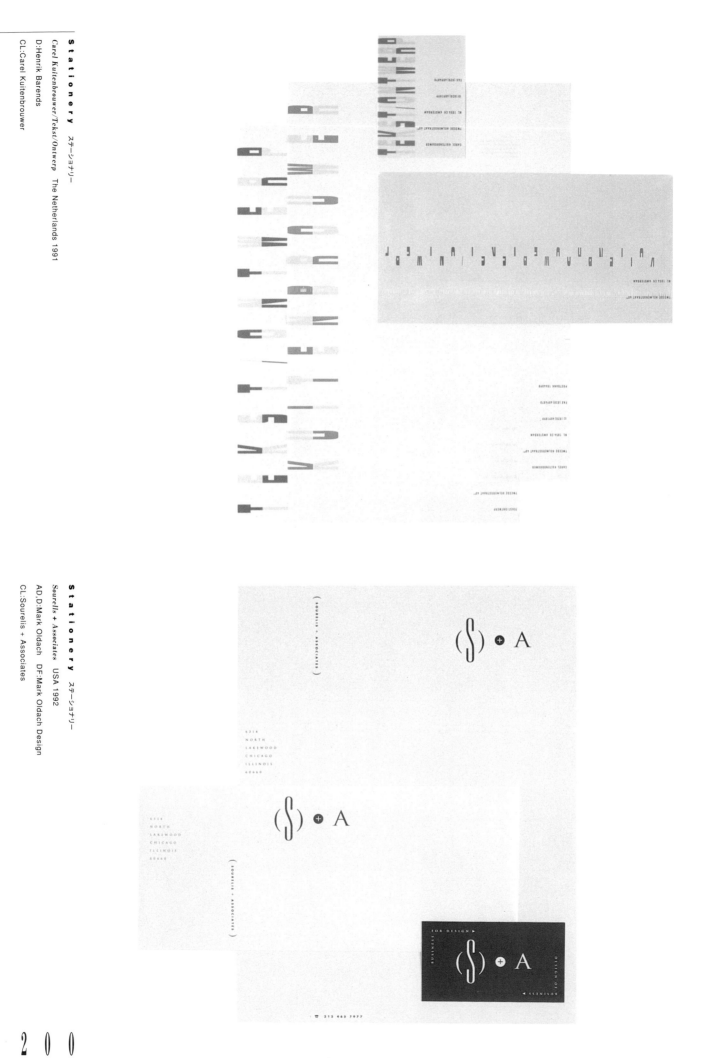

Stationery ステーショナリー

Carel Kuitenbrouwer/Tekst/Ontwerp The Netherlands 1991

D:Henrik Barends

CL:Carel Kuitenbrouwer

Stationery ステーショナリー

Sourelis + Associates USA 1992

AD,D:Mark Oldach DF:Mark Oldach Design

CL:Sourelis + Associates

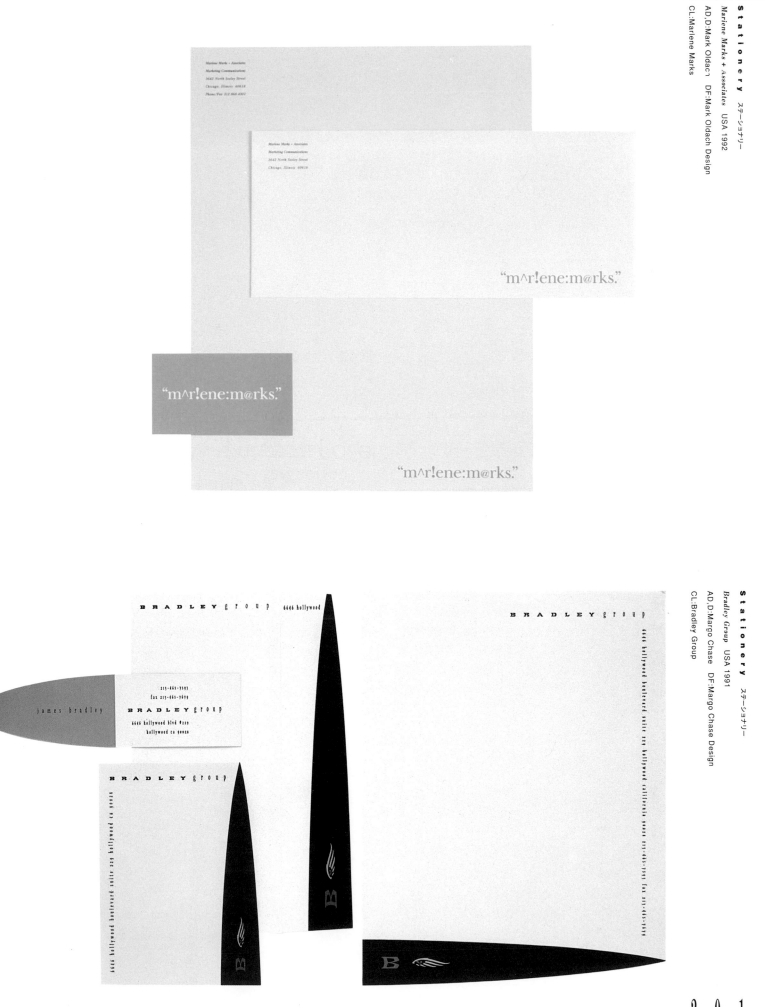

Stationery ステーショナリー

Marlene Marks + Associates USA 1992

AD.D:Mark Oldach DF:Mark Oldach Design

CL:Marlene Marks

Stationery ステーショナリー

Bradley Group USA 1991

AD.D:Margo Chase DF:Margo Chase Design

CL:Bradley Group

Stationery ステーショナリー

Lighthouse Grenada USA 1993

CD:Joel Fuller AD,D:Claudia Decastro

DF:Pinkhaus Design CL:Michael Magnuson, Lighthouse Grenaca

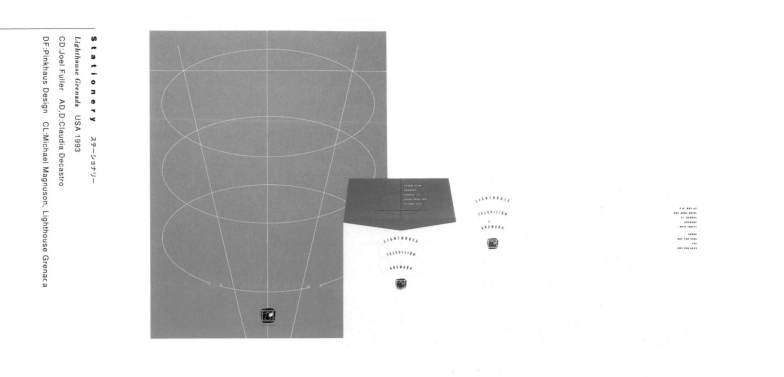

Stationery ステーショナリー

Cabra Diseño System USA 1992

D:Raul Cabra DF:Cabra Diseño

CL:Cabra Diseño

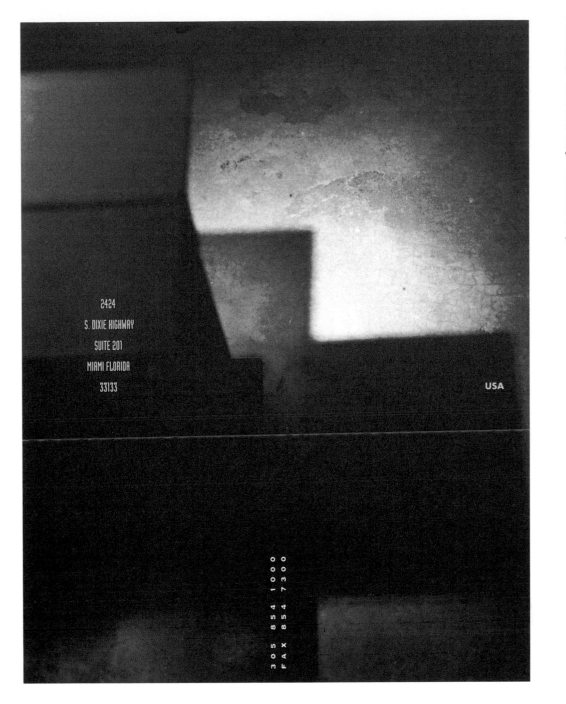

Stationery ステーショナリー

Pinkhaus Design USA 1991

CD.AD:Joel Fuller   AD:Mark Cantor   AD.D:Tom Sterling

P:Gallen Mei   DF:Pinkhaus Design   CL:Pinkhaus Design

2424
S. DIXIE HIGHWAY
SUITE 201
MIAMI FLORIDA
33133

USA

305 854 1000
FAX 854 7300

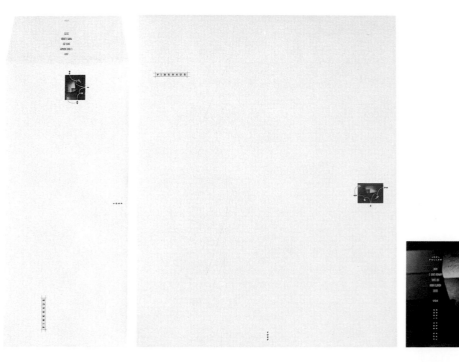

Stationery ステーショナリー

Typo Graphis　Japan 1992

AD,D:Tetsuyuki Kokin

CL:Typo Grapis

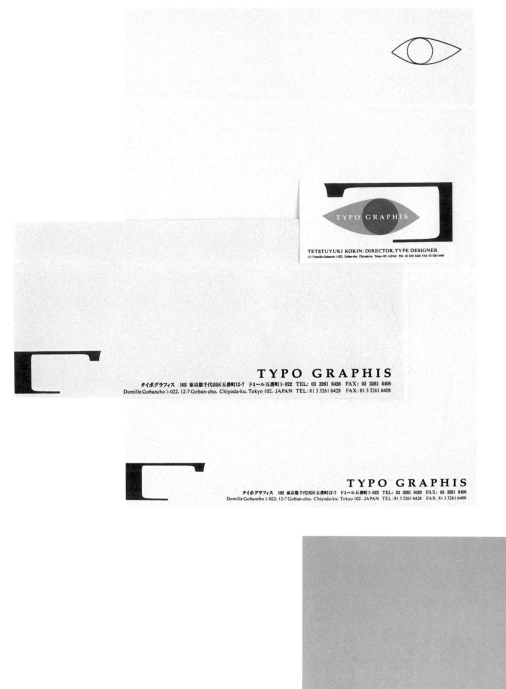

Letterhead レターヘッド

Presto　The Netherlands 1992

CD:Dick Launspach　D.I:Jaco Emmen

DF:Zwiers Partners　CL:Presto

Letterheads レターヘッド

Original Letterhead　Japan 1992
CD:Tsuyokatsu Kudo　AD,D,Artist:Tatsuomi Majima
D:Design Laboratory　DF:Design Laboratory　CL:Takeo

MAJIMA
TATSUOMI

Typographics "TEE" No.127 January February 10, 1991
Artist: Tatsuomi Majima
Paper: Iris Bond/TAKEO Co., Ltd.
Printing: Koyo Art Printing Co., Ltd.
Co-ordinator: Tsuyokatsu Kudo
Design: Tatsuomi Majima · Design Laboratory

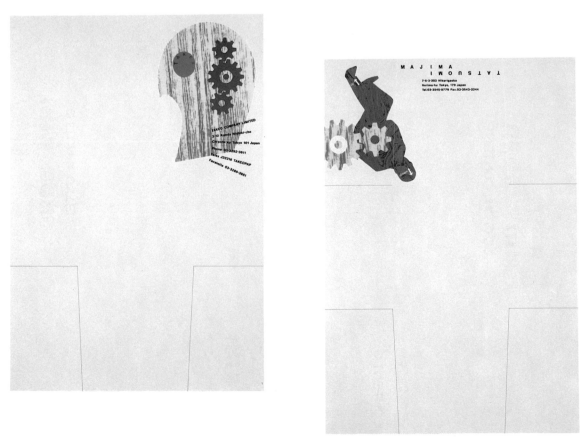

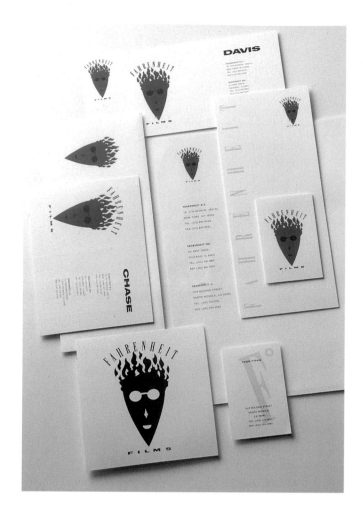

Stationery ステーショナリー
Fahrenheit USA 1992
AD.:Jay Vigon DF.:Jay Vigon Studio
CL.:Fahrenheit Film

Stationery ステーショナリー
Logo for The Cat Welfare Trust UK 1992
AD.D.I:Amelia Davies
DF:Bullitt CL:Cat Welfare Trust

WITH COMPLIMENTS

THE CAT
WELFARE
TRUST

4 - 6 PENEL ORLIEU
BRIDGWATER, SOMERSET, TA6 3PG
TELEPHONE 0278 427575
REGISTERED CHARITY NUMBER 800718

THE CAT
WELFARE
TRUST

4 - 6 PENEL ORLIEU, BRIDGWATER, SOMERSET, TA6 3PG, TELEPHONE 0278 427575
REGISTERED CHARITY NUMBER 800718

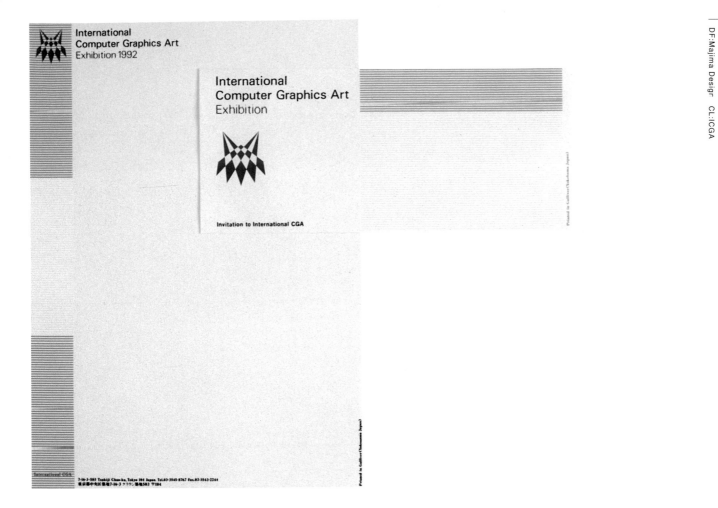

Stationery ステーショナリー

International Computer Graphics Art Exhibition　Japan 1992

AD,D:Tatsuomi Majima

DF:Majima Design　CL:ICGA

Stationery ステーショナリー

For Rex Three　USA 1990

CD,AD:Joel Fuller　AD,D:Lisa Ashworth　I:Ralf Schuetz

DF Pinkhaus Design　CL:Steve Miller, Rex Three

Stationery ステーショナリー

M　Finland 1993

AD.D:Ilkka Kärkkäinen　DF:Dynamo

CL:Mika Manninen

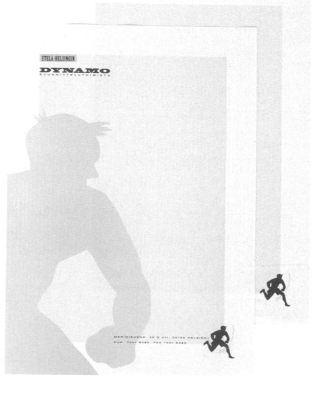

Stationery ステーショナリー

Dynamo　Finland 1992

AD:Ilkka Kärkkäinen　DF:Dynamo

CL:Dynamo

Stationery ステーショナリー

Theodor Finland 1993

AD:Ilkka Kärkkäiren

CL:Theodor

Stationery ステーショナリー

Orendo Finland 1993

AD,D:Ilkka Kärkkäir en　DF:Dynamo

CL:Orendo

Brochure and Stationery ブローシュア,ステーショナリー

MTV 3 Finland 1993

AD,D:Ilkka Kärkkäinen

CL:MTV 3

Magazine Spread 雑誌ページ

Symbolic Communication Japan 1992

AD,D:Koichi Yoshida

CL:Hakuhodo

TITLE DESIGN & ILLUSTRATION by Koichi Yoshida

JOB : KOUKOKUHI 7/1992
CLIENT : HAKUHODO
DESIGN by KOICHI YOSHIDA
SHELTER & GRAPHIC ASSOCIATES 1992
5P-4P

Flyer チラシ

COSA Japan 1993

AD,D:Koichi Yoshida

CL:Wave

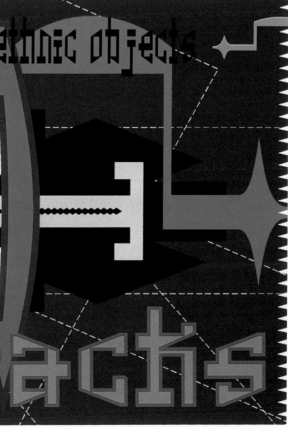

Sticker ステッカー

Flipper's Guitar:Doctor Head's World Tower Promotion Japan 1992

AD:Mitsuo Shindo D:Sawako Nakajima

DF:Contemporary Production CL:Polystar Records

Postcard ポストカード

American Crafts & Ethnic Objects USA 1992

AD,D,I:Carlos Segura

DF:Segura CL:Gimcracks

Promotional T-Shirt プロモーション用Tシャツ

Beautiful World Logo USA 1991

AD.D:Margo Chase DF:Margo Chase Design

CL:Margo Chase Design

Best of Austin 1992

Magazine Cover 雑誌カバー

Best of Austin USA 1992

AD:Ben Davis D:David Kampa I:David Kampa

DF:Kampa Design CL:Austin Chronicle

Magazine Spread 雑誌ページ

Logo type for "Best anc Worst" USA 1992

AD:Jim Darilek D:Liz Tindall

I:David Kampa DF:Kampa Design CL:D Magazine

Ten Inch Men

Record Packaging レコードパッケージ

Logotype for Ten Inch Men USA 1992
CD:Lisa Zambrano AD,D:Margo Chase
DF:Margo Chase Design CL:Victory Records

flea in Her EaR

Poster ポスター

Logotype for "A Flea in Her Ear" USA 1992
AD:Betty Wong, Oglivie + Mather(agency), Houston D:David Kampa
DF:Kampa Design CL:Alley Theatre

Greeting Card グリーティング・カード

Lois Levit USA 1992

AD,D:Michael McGinn AD:Takaaki Matsumoto

CL:Pratt Institute

The Herschel Levit Scholarship Fund
Pratt Institute
North Hall 219
200 Willoughby Avenue
Brooklyn, NY 11205

Book Cover ブックカバー

Kampa Books USA 1991

AD,D:David Kampa

DF:Kampa Design CL:Kampa Design

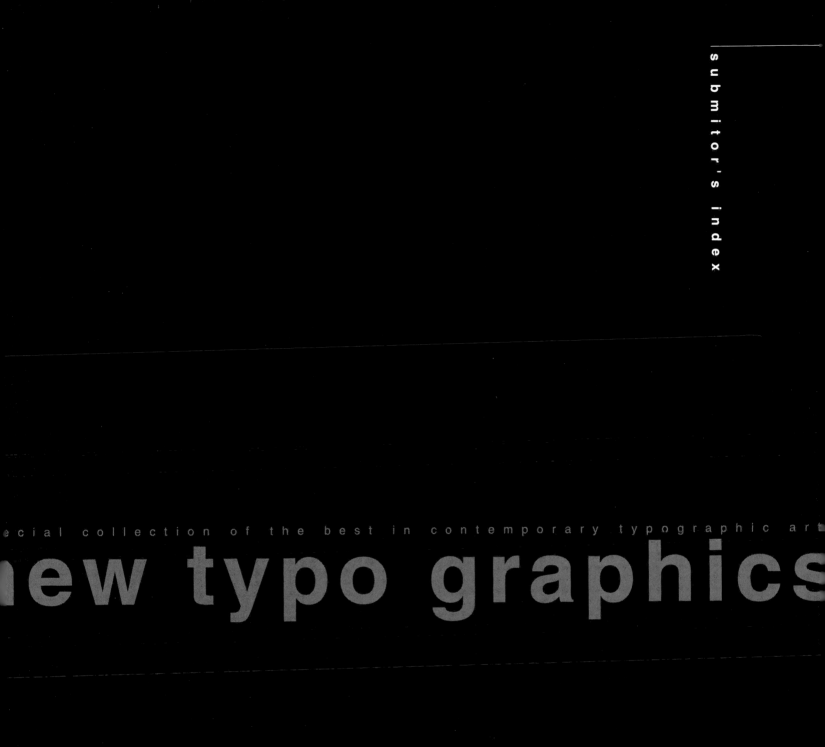

ecial collection of the best in contemporary typographic art

new typo graphics

P·I·E BOOKS

ecial collection of the best in contemporary typographic art

new typo graphics

new typo graphics
The new faces of contemporary typography

Art Director
Kazuo Abe
Designers
Kazuo Abe
Yutaka Ichimura
Miyuki Kawanabe
Masae Odajima
Editors
Kaori Shibata
Toru Hachiga
Photographer
Kuniharu Fujimoto
Coodinators
Masato Ieshiro (Tokyo)
Chizuko Gilmore (San Francisco)
Sarah Phillips (London)
English Translators & Advisers
Write Away Co.,LTD.
Douglas Allsopp
Eric Chaline
Publisher
Shingo Miyoshi

special collection of the best in contemporary typographic a

new typo graphics

1993年6月20日初版第1版発行

発行所　ピエ・ブックス
〒170 東京都豊島区駒込4-14-6-407
Tel:03-3949-5010 Fax:03-3949-5650

製版・印刷・製本　弘陽印刷
〒116 東京都荒川区東日暮里4-8-12
Tel:03-3802-1221 Fax:03-3801-9388

©1993 by P・I・E BOOKS

Printed in Japan

本書の収録内容の無断転載,複写,引用等を禁じます。
落丁乱丁はお取り替え致します。

ISBN 4-938586-43-6 C3070 P16000E

P·I·E Books, as always, has several new and ambitious graphic book projects in the works which will introduce a variety of superior designs from Japan and abroad. Currently we are planning the collection series detailed below. If you have any graphics which you consider worthy for submission to these publications, please fill in the necessary information on the inserted questionnaire postcard and forward it to us. You will receive a notice when the relevant project goes into production.

ピエ・ブックスでは、今後も新しいタイプの
グラフィック書籍の出版を目指すとともに、
国内外の優れたデザインを幅広く
紹介していきたいと考えております。
今後の刊行予定として下記のコレクション・シリーズを
企画しておりますので、
作品提供していただける企画がございましたら、
挟み込みのアンケートハガキに必要事項を記入の上
お送り下さい。企画が近づきましたら
そのつど案内書をお送りいたします。

A. POSTCARD GRAPHICS

A collection of various types of postcards including product advertising, direct mailers, invitations to events such as parties and fashion shows as well as birthday cards and seasonal greetings. In short all sorts of cards except the letter type which are mailed in envelopes.

A．ポストカード・グラフィックス

各シーズンのグリーティングカードをはじめとして、商品広告DM、パーティーやコレクション等のイベントのお知らせ、バースデイカードなど封書タイプを除く様々なポストカードをコレクションします。

B. ADVERTISING GREETING CARDS

A collection of letter-style direct mailers including sales promotional sheets, invitations to events such as exhibitions, parties and weddings. Some of these are quite simple, some have unusual shapes or dimensions (limited to cards inserted in envelopes).

B．アドバタイジング・グリーティングカード

販促用のDM、展示会・イベントの案内状やパーティや結婚式などの招待状など、プレーンなものから形状の変わったもの・立体になったものまで封書タイプのDMをコレクションします。（封書タイプのものに限ります）

C. BROCHURE & PAMPHLET COLLECTION

A collection of brochures and pamphlets categorized according to the business of the client company. Includes sales promotional pamphlets, product catalogues, corporate image brochures gallery exhibitions, special events, annual reports and company profiles from all sorts of businesses.

C．ブローシュア＆パンフレット・コレクション

販促用パンフレット、商品カタログ、イメージ・カタログ、ギャラリーや展示会・イベントのパンフレット、アニュアル・リポート、会社案内など様々な業種のブローシュアやパンフレットを業種別にコレクションします。

D. POSTER GRAPHICS

A collection of posters, classified according to the business of the client. Fashion, department stores, automotive, food, home appliances and almost any sort of poster you might see on streets. Invitational posters for art exhibitions, concerts and plays as well as regional posters which will be seen for the first time outside of the local area where they were published.

D．ポスター・グラフィックス

ファッション、デパート、車、食品、家電など街角を飾る広告ポスター、美術展、コンサート、演劇などのイベント案内ポスター、見る機会の少ない地方のポスターなどを業種別にコレクションします。

E. BOOK COVER AND EDITORIAL DESIGNS

Editorial and cover designs for various types of books and magazines. Includes all sorts of magazines, books, comics and other visual publications.

E．ブックカバー＆エディトリアル・デザイン

雑誌、単行本、ヴィジュアル書、コミックなど様々なタイプの書籍・雑誌のエディトリアル・デザイン、カバー・デザインを紹介します。

F. CORPORATE IMAGE LOGO DESIGNS

A collection of C.I. materials mainly symbols and logos for corporations of all sorts, classified according to the type of business. In some cases, development samples and trial comps as well as the final designs are included. Includes logos for magazines and various products.

F．コーポレイト・イメージ・ロゴマーク・デザイン

企業やショップのシンボルマーク・ロゴマークを中心に幅広い業種にわたり分類しコレクションします。マークのみではなく展開例としてのアプリケーションも数多く紹介し、その他、雑誌や商品などの様々なロゴマークもコレクションします。

G. BUSINESS CARD AND LETTERHEAD GRAPHICS

A collection of cards such as the business cards of corporations and individuals as well as shopping cards for restaurants and boutiques, membership cards and various prepaid cards. This collection centers on business cards, letterheads and shopping cards of superior design.

G．ビジネスカード＆レターヘッド・グラフィックス

様々な企業や個人の名刺、レストランやブティックのショップカード、会員カード、プリペイドカードなど、デザイン的に優れたカードを名刺・ショップカードを中心にコレクション。またカードのみでなくレターヘッドも紹介します。

H. CALENDAR GRAPHICS

A collection of visually interesting calendars. We do not take into account the form of the calendar, i.e. wall hanging-type or note-type or desktop-type etc. So that the calendars represent the widest range of possibilities.

H．カレンダー・グラフィックス

ヴィジュアル的に優れたカレンダーをコレクションします。壁掛けタイプ、ノートタイプ、ダイアリー、日めくりタイプ、卓上タイプなど形状にはこだわらず幅広い分野の様々なタイプのカレンダーを紹介します。

I. PACKAGE AND WRAPPING GRAPHICS

A collection of packaging and wrapping materials of superior design from Japan and abroad. Includes related accessories such as labels and ribbons and almost anything else that comes under the heading of containing, protecting and decorating things.

Ｉ．パッケージ＆ラッピング・グラフィックス

商品そのもののパッケージデザインはもちろん、いろいろな物を包む、保護する、飾るというコンセプトで国内外の優れたパッケージ、ケース、ラッピング・デザイン及びラベル、リボンなどの付属アクセサリー類を幅広く紹介します。

Comme toujours, P·I·E Books a dans ses ateliers plusieurs projets de livres graphiques neufs et ambitieux qui introduiront une gamme de modèles supérieurs en provenance du Japon et de l'étranger. Nous prévoyons en ce moment la série de collections détaillée ci-dessous. Si vous êtes en possession d'un graphique que vous jugez digne de soumettre à ces publications, nous vous prions de remplir les informations nécessaires sur l'étiquette à renvoyer située à la carte postale questionnaire insérée et de nous la faire parvenir. Vous recevrez un avis lorsque le projet correspondant passera à la production.

Wie immer hat P·I·E Books einige neue anspruchsvolle Grafikbücher in Arbeit, die eine Vielzahl von hervorragenden Designs aus Japan und anderen Ländern vorstellen werden. Momentan planen wir eine Serie mit den nachfolgend aufgeführten Themen.
Wenn Sie grafische Darstellungen besitzen, von denen Sie meinen, daß sie in diese Veröffentlichung aufgenommen werden könnten, geben Sie uns bitte die nötigen Informationen auf der entsprechenden Antwortseite am füllen Sie die beigelegte Antwortkarte aus und schicken Sie sie an uns. Wir werden Sie benachrichtigen, wenn das entsprechende Projekt in Arbeit geht.

A. Graphiques pour cartes postales
Une collection de divers types de cartes postales, y compris la publicité de produits, l'adressage direct, des invitations à des événements tels que soirées et défilés de mode, ainsi que des cartes d'anniversaire et des voeux de saison. En bref, toutes sortes de cartes, à part le type lettre qui sera envoyé dans des enveloppes.

B. Cartes de voeux publicitaires
Une collection d'adressages directs style lettre y compris des feuilles de promotion de ventes, des invitations à des événements tels qu'expositions, soirées et mariages. Certaines d'entre elles sont très simples, d'autres ont des formes ou dimensions inhabituelles (limitées aux cartes insérées dans des enveloppes).

C. Collection de brochures et de pamphlets
Une collection de brochures et de pamphlets triées en fonction des affaires de la société client. Comprend des pamphlets de promotion des ventes, des catalogues de produits, des brochures sur l'image de la société, des expositions de galerie, des événements spéciaux, des compte-rendus annuels et des profils de sociétés de toutes sortes d'affaires.

D. Graphiques sur affiche
Une collection d'affiches, classées en fonction du secteur d'affaires du client. La mode, les grands magasins, l'automobile, l'alimentation, les appareils électro-ménagers et presque tous les types d'affiche que vous pouvez voir dans les rues. Des affiches invitant à des expositions d'art, des concerts et des pièces ainsi que des affiches régionales qui seront vues pour la première fois en dehors de la région où elles ont été éditées.

E. Designs de couverture de livre et d'éditorial
Des designs de livre et d'éditorial de divers types de livres et magazines. Comprend toutes sortes de magazines, livres, bandes dessinées et autres publications visuelles.

F. Designs de logo d'image de société
Une collection de matériaux d'image de société, principalement des symboles et des logos pour sociétés de toutes sortes ; classés en fonction du type d'affaires. Dans certains cas, sont inclus des échantillons de développement et également des compositions d'essai ainsi que les designs finaux. Comprend des logos pour magazines et divers produits.

G. Graphiques pour en-têtes et cartes de visite
Une collection de cartes telles que les cartes de visite de sociétés et d'individus ainsi que les cartes de fidélité de restaurants et de boutiques, les cartes de membre et diverses cartes payées à l'avance. Cette collection se concentre sur les cartes de visite, les en-têtes et les cartes de fidélité d'une qualité supérieure.

H. Graphiques pour calendrier
Une collection de calendriers visuellement intéressants. Nous ne tenons pas compte de la forme du calendrier, c.-à-d., type à accrocher au mur, type carnet ou type bureau, etc. de telle sorte que les calendriers représentent la gamme de possibilités la plus large.

I. Graphiques pour emballage et paquetage
Une collection de matériaux d'emballage et de paquetage de qualité supérieure en provenance du Japon et de l'étranger. Comprend des accessoires en relation tels qu'étiquettes et rubans, et presque tout ce qui est destiné à contenir, protéger et décorer des choses.

A. Postkarten-Grafik
Zusammenstellung verschiedener Postkartenarten, und zwar für Produktwerbung, Direkt Mailing, Einladungen zu Parties und Modenschauen sowie Geburtstagskarten und Karten zu verschiedenen Jahreszeiten. Also alle Arten von Karten, ausgenommen Briefkarten.

B. Werbe-Grußkarten
Zusammenstellung briefähnlicher Direkt-Mailings, wie z.B. verkaufsfördernde Texte, Einladungen zu Anlässen wie Ausstellungen, Parties oder Hochzeiten. Einige von ihnen sind recht einfach gemacht, andere fallen durch ungewöhnliches Aussehen oder Größe auf (Karten dürfen Umschlaggröße nicht überschreiten).

C. Zusammenstellung von Broschüren und Druckschriften
Diese Zusammenstellung von Broschüren und Druckschriften ist nach den Tätigkeiten der Kundenfirmen geordnet. Sie beinhaltet verkaufsfördernde Broschüren, Produktkataloge, Corporate-Image-Broschüren, Galerieausstellungen, besondere Veranstaltungen und Firmenprofile für alle Arten von Unternehmen.

D. Postergrafik
Eine Zusammenstellung von Postern, die nach dem Geschäftsgebiet des Kunden geordnet sind. Mode Kaufhäuser, Kraftfahrzeuge, Nahrungsmittel, Haushaltsgeräte und fast jede Art von Postern, die auf der Straße zu sehen sind. Einladungsposter für Kunstausstellungen, Konzerte und Theaterstücke ebenso wie Poster mit regionalen Themen, die zum ersten Mal außerhalb des Gebietes, in dem sie aufgehängt wurden, zu sehen sein werden.

E. Bucheinbände und redaktionelles Design
Bucheinbände und redaktionelles Design für verschiedenste Buch- und Zeitschriftentypen. Dies schließt alle Arten von Zeitschriften, Büchern, Comics und anderen visuellen Publikationen ein.

F. Corporate-Image-Logo-Design
Dies ist eine Zusammenstellung von C.I.-Material, und zwar hauptsächlich von Symbolen und Logos für Firmen aller Art, nach Geschäftsgebieten geordnet. In manchen Fällen sind die Arbeiten der Entwicklungsphase und Probeexemplare ebenso miteinbezogen wie das endgültige Design. Logos für Zeitschriften und andere Produkte sind miteingeschlossen.

G. Visitenkarten und Briefkopt-Grafik
Dies ist eine Zusammenstellung verschiedener Visitenkarten, z.B. für Firmen und Einzelpersonen, Kreditkarten für Restaurants und Boutiquen, Mitgliedskarten und Vorverkaufskarten. Diese Sammlung konzentriert sich vor allem auf geschäftliche Karten, Briefköpfe und Geschäftseigene Kreditkarten mit herausragendem Design.

H. Kalendergrafik
Eine Zusammenstellung von optisch interessanten Kalendern. Es ist für uns dabei unwichtig, ob es sich um die Form des Wandkalenders, Tischkalenders oder Notizbuchkalenders handelt, sodaß die größtmögliche Vielfalt an Kalendern gezeigt werden kann.

I. Grafik auf Verpackungen und Verpackungsmaterial
Eine Zusammenstellung von Grafik auf Verpackungen und Verpackungsmaterial mit herausragendem Design aus Japan und anderen Ländern. Dazugehörige Accessoires wie Etiketten und Bänder sind eingeschlossen, ebenso wie fast alles, was als Behälter für Produkte dienen kann, sie ziert oder schützt.

ADVERTISING GREETING CARDS 1
Pages: 224(144 in color) ¥15,000
業種別ダイレクトメールの集大成
A collection of more than 500 direct mail pieces selected from thousands used throughout Japan. Cards were selected for their distinctive design and include 3-D pop-ups, special die-cuts, folds and embossings.

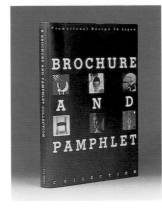

BROCHURE & PAMPHLET COLLECTION 1
Pages: 224(144 in color) ¥15,000
業種別カタログ・コレクション
Here are hundreds of the best brochures and pamphlets from Japan.
This collection will make a valuable sourcebook for anyone involved in corporate identity advertising and graphic design.

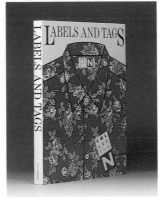

LABELS AND TAGS
Pages: 224(192 in color) ¥15,000
ファッションのラベル＆タグ・コレクション
Over 1,600 garment labels representing 450 brands produced in Japan are included in this full-color collection.

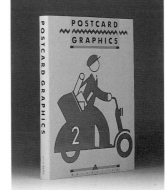

POSTCARD GRAPHICS 2
Pages: 240(208 in color) ¥16,000
好評！業種別ポストカードの第2弾
Here are 1,500 promotional postcards created by Japan's top design talent. A wide range of clients are represented including 120 fashion houses and 90 major retailers. Presented in striking full color.

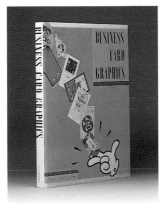

BUSINESS CARD GRAPHICS 1
Pages: 256(160 in color) ¥16,000
世界の名刺＆ショップカード集大成
Over 1,200 business cards are presented in this international collection.
Created by 500 of the world's top design firms, designers will discover a wealth of new ideas in this remarkable collection.

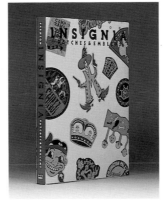

FASHION INSIGNIA
Pages: 224(208 in color) ¥16,000
ファッションのワッペン・コレクション
One thousand full-color emblems have been gathered in this beautiful and sometimes playful collection.
The great variety of color and shape demonstrates the versatility of embroidery art.

ADVERTISING GREETING CARDS 2
Pages: 224(176 in color) ¥16,000
世界のダイレクトメール・コレクション
500 visually remarkable works representing a variety of businesses. Pieces include new product announcements, invitation cards and direct mail envelopes. An excellent image bank for graphic designers.

BROCHURE DESIGN FORUM 1
Pages: 224(192 in color) ¥15,000
世界のカタログ・コレクション
A large collection of international brochures from a variety of business categories. Showcases more than 250 eye-catching works.

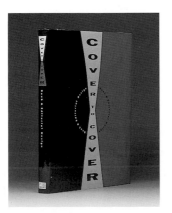

COVER TO COVER
Pages: 240(176 in color) ¥17,000
世界のブック＆エディトリアル・デザイン
The latest trends in book and magazine design are illustrated with over 1,000 creative works by international firms.

BUSINESS STATIONERY GRAPHICS 1
Pages: 224(192 in color) ¥15,000
世界のレターヘッド・コレクション
Creatively designed letterheads, business cards, memo pads, and other business forms and documents are included this international collection.

MUSIGRAPHICS 1
Pages: 224(192 in color) ¥16,000
世界のＬＰ＆ＣＤグラフィックス
A collection of more than 600 of the world's most outstanding CD and LP covers, featuring design for all musical genres.

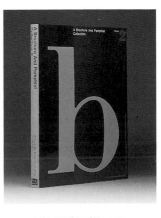

BROCHURE & PAMPHLET COLLECTION 2
Pages: 224(192 in color) ¥15,000
業種別カタログ・コレクション、第2弾
Features a selection of 1,000 brochures and pamphlets covering a wide range of products from Japan. The value of brochures in visual communication is demonstrated in this dazzling collection.

CORPORATE IMAGE DESIGN
Pages: 336(272 in color) ¥16,000
世界の業種別CI・ロゴマーク
This collection presents the best
corporate identity projects from around
the world. Creative and effective designs
from top international firms are featured
in this valuable source book.

POSTCARD GRAPHICS 3
Pages: 232(208 in color) ¥16,000
世界の業種別ポストカード・コレクション
Volume 3 in the series presents more
than 1,200 promotional postcards in
dazzling full color. Top designers from
the world over have contributed to this
useful image bank of ideas.

**GRAPHIC BEAT
LONDON/TOKYO 1 & 2**
Pages: 224(208 in color) ¥16,000
音楽とグラフィックのコラボレーション
1,500 music-related graphic works from
29 of the hottest designers in Tokyo and
London. Features Malcolm Garrett,
Russell Miles, Tadanori Yokoo, Neville
Brody, Vaughn Oliver and others.

The Creative Index ARTIFILE
Pages: 224(Full color) ¥12,500
実力派プロダクション104社の作品集
Showcases the best works from 104
graphic studios in Japan and abroad.
A variety of fields included such as
advertising design, corporate identity,
photography and illustration.

CALENDAR GRAPHICS
Pages: 224(192 in color) ¥16,000
世界のカレンダー・グラフィックス
An exciting collection of creatively
designed calendars from around the
world. A wide variety of styles included
such as poster, book and 3-D calendars.
Clients range from large corporations to
retail shops.

BUSINESS CARD GRAPHICS 2
Pages: 224(192 in color) ¥16,000
世界の名刺&ショップカード、第2弾
This latest collection presents 1,000
creative cards from international
designers. Features hundreds of cards
used in creative fields such as graphic
design and architecture.

T-SHIRT GRAPHICS
Pages: 224(192 in color) ¥16,000
世界のTシャツ・グラフィックス
This unique collection showcases 700
wonderfully creative T-Shirt designs from
the world's premier design centers.
Grouped according to theme, categories
include sports, casual, designer and
promotional shirts among others.

DIAGRAM GRAPHICS
Pages: 224(192 in color) ¥16,000
世界のダイアグラム・デザインの集大成
Hundreds of unique and lucid diagrams,
charts, graphs, maps and technical
illustrations from leading international
design firms. Variety of media
represented including computer graphics.

SPECIAL EVENT GRAPHICS
Pages: 224(192 in color) ¥16,000
世界のイベント・グラフィックス特集
This innovative collection features design
elements from concerts, festivals, fashion
shows, symposiums and more.
International works include posters,
tickets, flyers, invitations and various
premiers.

PACKAGING DESIGN & GRAPHICS 1
Pages: 224(192 in color) ¥16,000
世界の業種別パッケージ・デザイン
An international collection featuring 400
creative and exciting package designs
from renowned designers.

RETAIL IDENTITY GRAPHICS
Pages: 208(176 in color) ¥14,800
世界のショップ・グラフィックス
This visually exciting collection
showcases the identity design campaigns
of restaurants, bars, shops and various
other retailers. Wide variety of pieces are
featured including business cards, signs,
menus, bags and hundreds more.

ADVERTISING GREETING CARDS 3
Pages: 224(176 in color) ¥16,000
世界のダイレクトメール集大成、第3弾
The best-selling series continues with
this collection of elegantly designed
advertising pieces from a wide variety of
categories. This exciting image bank of
ideas will interest all graphic designers
and direct mail specialists.